Robert M. Reach brilliantly weaves his ex
dations. He gives the readers an overview
illustrations that have worked over the dec

Movement Catalyst; Author, *Acts and the Movement of God*

For years, mission-focused leaders have looked in awe at the Acts of the Apostles, hoping to glean understanding into how to effectively fulfill the Great Commission. Through prayer, fasting, and personal surrender, the Lord has helped Robert Reach discover what has been right in front of the church for centuries—the Book of Acts was not the beginning of the radical discipleship movement of the early church. Christ himself was the first practitioner of making multiplying disciples. The Gospels are the template for a multiplying Jesus movement. Reach and his network of movement leaders have faithfully applied, learned, and improved on the best practices of our Lord Jesus. The fruit is real, multiplying, and God-glorifying.

I personally pray that there is a global revival of obedience and faithfulness to following in the steps of Jesus to make multiplying disciples. I believe that the principles shared herein are a key piece of the puzzle. I pray that they will be read, understood, and applied to God's glory.

MATT BRENNAN
CEO, DIR Holdings, LLC & GROVE

If you desire a real firsthand feel of what Jesus is up to in cities, villages, neighborhoods, and families around the globe—through faithful disciple-makers on the ground—you need to read Robert M. Reach's *Impacting Eternity*. The stories throughout this book will inspire and deeply move you; the root principles revealed behind disciple-making movements will be transformative for you; and the thrust of this book will leave you challenged to discover how Jesus wants to move through you. A must-read for every disciple of Jesus that wants to make a real difference!

DAVE BUEHRING
Founder and President, Lionshare; Author, *A Discipleship Journey*

Beginning with a brief history of "movements," Robert Reach summarizes core principles gleaned and lessons learned from his work in facilitating movements, from inception to sustained expansion. *Impacting Eternity* is indeed "A Practitioner's Guide." It is written by a seasoned practitioner who has been in the trenches, not an academician theorizing from an ivory tower. Reach's book is grounded, not just in his experience around the world (both the successes and failures), but also in research he has conducted and the study of data he has gathered over several decades. He advocates empowering new believers to take ownership of evangelism and discipleship within their cultural context.

I commend this book to those wanting to come alongside new believers and leaders in a manner that may result in a movement, so that they, in turn, can "get out of the way" as the Lord brings the increase.

MYRON F. GOODWIN, PhD
Missions Pastor, Grace Chapel, Franklin, TN

Having known Robert Reach for over ten years and having been involved in investigating the principles in his book "in the field" of Southeast Asia, I have seen firsthand the fruit that is supported by the seven root factors and best leadership principles he describes. It is undeniable that this Jesus Movement he reveals, and the spirit-led strategy that is unpacked in this book, will serve as a wise counsel for those willing to humbly look beyond the traditional Western approaches and tap into the power of this incredible movement of God.

JAMES J. JEROZAL, JR.
International Impact Pastor
Christ Community Church, South Elgin/St. Charles, IL

The love language of a Disciple Making Movement (DMM) is healthy and rapid multiplication of disciples, leaders, intercessors, small groups, and churches. This is the reason why I am calling passionate practitioners to join me in endorsing *Impacting Eternity*. With more than thirty years' personal experience as a DMM Trainer, Coach, and Practitioner, I endorse the content of the book because of its creativity, simplicity, and the intentionality of the author in laying out kingdom principles that catalyze the rapid multiplication of disciples and disciple-makers.

The book provides an insight into Jesus movements, the fresh 5-5-5 methodology, the Fruit, Roots, Branches of movements, and most importantly, the recommended 7 leadership best practices. The cited examples and stories can be applicable to every disciple-making culture around the world.

Rev SHODANKEH JOHNSON
New Harvest Ministries, Sierra Leone, West Africa

Robert Reach uses the Bible as the basis for emphasizing the power of the Holy Spirit. With this power, every disciple can fulfill Jesus's Great Commission by training, developing, and multiplying disciples.

YING KAI
Training for Trainers (T4T) Founder

Robert Reach has taken the best ideas of modern missiologists, his own research of the great movements of the past twenty-five years, and the personal experience of seeing a large movement birthed—to show what God is continuing to do today. New chapters of the Spirit's work are being written even now as they were two thousand years ago in the Book of Acts.

RANDALL KENNEDY
Senior Strategy Director, The Maclellan Foundation, Inc.

Robert Reach is a remarkable individual who epitomizes the principles he teaches and walks out in faith. As a fellow member of the board of directors, I have witnessed his unwavering commitment to his mission to advance the gospel. Personally, I had the privilege of visiting a house church in Asia, where I listened to their stories, prayed for them in the face of persecution, and saw the transformative impact of Robert's methods. His approach combines tested strategies with adaptable flexibility, enabling seamless integration into diverse cultural contexts. Robert's work is truly effective, proven, and embodies the perfect balance of structure and adaptability.

MATT MCCAULEY
CEO LogoBrands, Franklin, TN

As someone who has journeyed with Robert Reach and his team's ministry these past twenty years on two continents, I can testify to the stunning fruitfulness the Lord has wrought. This is due in no small part to applying the learnings, practices, and support systems described in this book. We all have to decide how we are going to relate to something new we see the Lord doing.

I commend this book to you to gain a deeper insight into this new paradigm called movement.

BRETT NORDICK
The R. B. Nordick Foundation

If the modern church has proven anything, it's that our preaching, programs, and piety are not enough to bring the gospel to the ends of the earth. In Impacting Eternity, we're not given mere rhetoric or theory, but a tested and proven strategy for multiplicative discipleship that has already been effectively reaching both Western and Eastern cultures for over fifteen years.

In the following pages, you will find a powerful convergence of real-world research and kingdom principles that are both comprehensive and applicable in any context around the globe. If you want to see the Spirit of God begin a movement of multiplicative discipleship in your part of the world, a movement that will live longer and reach farther than you can imagine, God has given you a gift in Robert Reach's work. This book is for you.

ROB ROGERS
Pastor, Grace Chapel, Franklin, TN

I've known Robert Reach for over thirty years as an active board member of his ministry. I've travelled with him, prayed with him, and seen his life up close and personal. I also know the leaders in his movements. I've watched these movements grow and develop from an idea into a huge reality, like the mustard seed becoming a massive tree. This book reveals the inner workings of the Spirit as he led Robert, step-by-step, in ways that often contradicted the Western worldview of how the kingdom grows. Let the Spirit speak to you as you read this book and confirm in your heart what will impact eternity in your life and context.

HARRY SHIELDS
Former Owner, International Computer Sales and Service Companies

Robert Reach's book is well documented, thoroughly researched, globally helpful, and powerfully practical for anyone desiring to be used by God to usher large numbers of lost to salvation through multiplying disciples.

As a rigorous researcher, hands-on practitioner, and historian familiar with past century seminal movement thinkers, he is uniquely qualified to systemize root principles operative from the book of Acts to modern-day South Asia.

I have known Robert for decades. From South Asia to West Africa, key local apostles follow his guidance, implement his root principles, and praise God that a Westerner clothed in humility never demands credit or puts his real name on what so obviously is a genuine fruitful work of the Holy Spirit.

BILL SMITH
Movement Practitioner, Trainer, Coach, and Former Strategy Coordinator

It has been said that four ingredients are necessary to start a movement: 1) dissatisfaction with the current system; 2) knowledge of a better way; 3) known first steps; and 4) possessing the first three in greater proportion than the inertia of the status quo. If that's true, then Robert Reach has provided all the necessary ingredients used by the Spirit of God to produce and sustain disciple-making movements around the globe. That's exciting!

TERRY TIEMAN
Transforming Churches Network

Having served on the board of Robert Reach's mission organization for fifteen years, I have witnessed firsthand as the Lord has inspired and led Robert's movement work. Robert is uniquely gifted with a nimbleness and sensitivity to the Holy Spirit that allows the Lord to both use and flow through him to grow his kingdom. The exponential inspiration of the 5-5-5 strategy is nothing short of groundbreaking. Robert's style of equipping crosses cultural barriers by embracing the culture of each community and its unique connection to Christ. I have been immensely blessed to watch Robert's movements and strategy grow and have no doubt, regardless of your stage or position in life or in the ministry, this book will bless you as well.

JINANNE WEST
Chairperson and Board Member

Impacting Eternity

A Practitioner's Guide for Sustained Movement Expansion

Robert M. Reach

WILLIAM
CAREY
PUBLISHING

Available at missionbooks.org

Published by William Carey Publishing
10 W. Dry Creek Cir
Littleton, CO 80120 | www.missionbooks.org

William Carey Publishing is a ministry of Frontier Ventures
Pasadena, CA | www.frontierventures.org

Cover and Interior Designer: Mike Riester

ISBNs: 978-1-64508-487-7 (paperback)
       978-1-64508-489-1 (epub)

Printed Worldwide

27 26 25 24 23   1 2 3 4 5   IN

Library of Congress data on file with the publisher.

Contents

Foreword by Curtis Sergeant   viii

Preface   x

Chapter 1: A Look Inside Jesus Movements   1

Chapter 2: A New Testament Jesus Movement   15

Chapter 3: Roland Allen: A Prophet of Modern Jesus Movements   27

Chapter 4: Donald McGavran: A Father of Modern Movements   39

Chapter 5: Understanding How Movements Work   49

Chapter 6: The Root Principles   59

Chapter 7: Leadership Best Practice #1:
Depend upon the Presence and Power of the Spirit   73

Chapter 8: Leadership Best Practice #2:
Catalyze a Decentralized Movement   89

Chapter 9: Leadership Best Practice #3:
Learning Communities Develop New Leaders   105

Chapter 10: Leadership Best Practice #4:
Foster Obedience-Based Discipleship   117

Chapter 11: Leadership Best Practice #5:
Empower God's Saints for Works of Service   129

Chapter 12: Leadership Best Practice #6:
Foster a Self-Supporting System   141

Chapter 13: Leadership Best Practice #7:
Develop Patterns That Are Reproducible   157

Chapter 14: Next Steps   167

Bibliography   171

Appendix: A Comprehensive Listing
of References to Jesus ('Isa) in the Qur'an   175

Foreword

Robert Reach's life is a constant encouragement to me. He is a rare example of a missions researcher and consultant from a very traditional background who became an extremely fruitful and effective practitioner of kingdom-movement approaches. He was intrigued by seemingly incredible reports from early practitioners in such movements and decided to look into them in an up close and personal way.

After hundreds of interviews in various countries and among various movements, Robert analyzed the results with statistical rigor and identified a number of factors that were common among movements and that set them apart from more traditional approaches. He became convinced that the effectiveness of the approaches was not dependent upon people who had outstanding gifts or unusual skill sets. He desperately wanted to experience the kind of fruitfulness he had observed in his research.

Robert decided to attempt to replicate what he had observed in a large, unreached, predominantly Muslim nation with very few Christians and yet with significant persecution. I believe his choice of "targets" was fortuitous, because in many ways his choice presented more of a blank slate, which avoided some of the common barriers that often arise in cultures with more of a historically "Christian" background.

The outcome has been remarkable. The result has been what is very likely the largest single movement among Muslims anywhere and one of the top ten movements among any type of population in any nation. Robert has since begun to replicate these results among other people groups in other nations.

I have known Robert since the days of his initial interest in movements. I appreciated his focus and passion and dedication, but I was mildly concerned that he might be perceiving movements from a bit too much of a clinical, sociological perspective. If there were any hints of that in his early work, however, they are gone now. While it was the quantitative advantages of movement approaches that first drew Robert's attention, he now clearly recognizes that the qualitative advantages are more significant. Better and stronger disciples tend to result from these approaches. This is clear in any conversation with him today, and that conviction comes through in this volume.

This book makes helpful contributions to the literature on movements. To begin with, it is written by a successful practitioner. I personally value this characteristic. Many movement books are written by those who have tagged along and participated in the work of others and written about it. There is nothing wrong with that, but there is an added dimension to books written by the primary catalyst of a movement.

Another important contribution is the fact that Robert addresses structural issues. Many people within the "movement world" seem to be allergic to structure. They view the organic nature of movements to be incompatible with structure, and they see the two as diametrically opposed. This is absolutely incorrect. Certain types or expressions of structure may be in tension with movement principles, but the natural world is full of structure. Structure need not hinder organic growth; and it can, in fact, enable such growth to scale to larger sizes.

An additional aspect of structure that sometimes offends some people in the movement world is that they view structure as being opposed to following the leadership of the Holy Spirit at the individual and corporate levels. Of course, this could be true if one applied structure inappropriately, but this need not be the case. In fact, it is clear that God works through structure in his church and among his people—in addition to guiding them moment by moment both individually and corporately. Robert helps illustrate what this can look like in actual practice.

The final contribution of this book that I will mention is the fact that it clearly addresses issues related to finances in movements. This is an issue that is rarely addressed in any depth in most movement books and which I myself have not addressed nearly enough. Nearly everyone recognizes that the minimal overhead expenses in movements allows them to be far more efficient in their use of funds. Robert unpacks some of that topic.

I pray that many who read this book will be sparked to begin a journey similar to Robert's. Even if you are not called to seek to catalyze a new movement, I pray that the Lord will draw you into applying these principles in your own context and supporting others who are doing so. May the result be that we all become more and more effective in making disciples who multiply.

—CURTIS SERGEANT

Preface

Welcome to *Impacting Eternity: A Practitioner's Guide for Sustained Movement Expansion*. This book is a culmination of my years of experience working in the field of movement growth, having facilitated three large movements, as well as my passion for empowering others to make a lasting impact on the world.

As a practitioner in the field, I have seen firsthand the transformative power of the 5-5-5 methodology and sustained movement expansion practices. It is not just about short-term growth or success, but rather about building a foundation for lasting impact that can continue for generations to come.

This book is written for anyone who desires to make a significant impact on the world and is willing to put in the time and effort to make it happen. Whether you are a movement practitioner, a pastor, a missionary, a community leader, or simply someone with a heart for making a difference, this book will provide you with practical strategies and insights for achieving sustained movement expansion.

Throughout this book, I will share with you the key principles and practices that have helped me and others to make a lasting impact on the world. I will discuss topics such as the seven Root Principles that create the hidden dynamics that fuel massive growth and also the seven leadership best practices that sustain the growth over multiple generations.

I want to thank my life partner, Linda, for her loving support and extensive travel with me over these past decades to see this prayer for impact become a reality. She has been, and is, a rock in my life and that of our three daughters and seven grandchildren.

I could not have written this book without the help of M. Scott Boren. Scott has worked hard on crafting the book, doing background research on the historical mission thinkers I have written about and helped shape the whole book. Thank you, Scott!

These massive movements and this book are a result of three things: The final command of Christ to make disciple makers, the prayer for help to fulfill that command, and the passion to obey. Hundreds of thousands exhibit this life and are seeing God transform lives. All glory to our gracious and loving Father!

My hope is that this book will inspire and empower you to take action and make a lasting impact on the world around you. Whether you are just starting out on your journey or are looking for ways to take your impact to the next level, *Impacting Eternity* will provide you with the tools and guidance you need to make a sustained difference in the world.

—Robert M. Reach

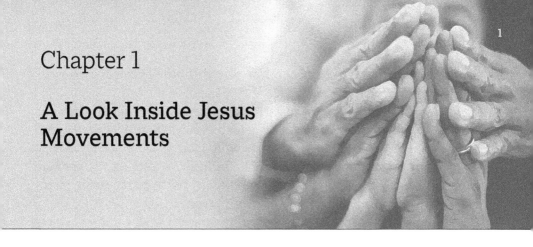

Chapter 1

A Look Inside Jesus Movements

God's movements are a result of Jesus's life moving through God's people. The evidence is in. If you are willing, look at what God is doing through movements, about how he is changing lives—not by the tens, or even by the hundreds, or even by the thousands. Jesus movements are changing neighborhoods, villages, towns, and cities by the *hundreds of thousands*, each with a unique story of what God is doing.

Take Haja, for instance, a town chief in West Africa who was also a devout Muslim. He learned about Jesus from a man from a nearby village who visited his town. Haja knew that Jesus is referred to in the Qur'an. Mentioning Jesus in over ninety verses, Islam corroborates that he was born to a virgin, was sinless, performed miracles, and was superior to other prophets. Yet Islam teaches that Jesus was no more than a prophet.

> Within twenty-four hours, he had led eight other Muslims to Jesus and baptized them.

Haja learned, from the disciple-maker who shared with him, that none of us can go to heaven unless we put our whole trust in Jesus. After considering the matter, Haja eventually received Jesus as his Savior and was baptized a few days later. Within twenty-four hours, he had led eight other Muslims to Jesus and baptized them, along with most of his household. A church currently meets in Haja's home three times a week.

We are living in a time when the rate of people being reached with the gospel exceeds what is recorded in the book of Acts. When I share with church leaders about these results, I've yet to find one who does not want to experience them firsthand. However, most fail—for various reasons—to come anywhere close to movement life. I want to suggest that there are times and seasons when the Spirit of God sovereignly blesses a people or nations. In the US, we experienced the well-documented Jesus Movement in the 1960s to 80s. Another Jesus movement, which surpasses our hopes and dreams, is happening around the world today.

We pray for the harvest and for more workers and fruit in the Western world; and many leaders are trying to apply movement principles, with some success. This takes wisdom and strategic insight, along with prayer and hard work. Perhaps this book can add to the literature seeking to empower workers in all walks of life and in all interested nations to become more adept at working with the Holy Spirit to reap the harvest of God.

The challenge of understanding how movements work became clear to me in a conversation with a missions pastor from a large church here in the US. He was an experienced missionary who had served for two decades in Africa. As we talked over lunch, I shared with him some of the data about our movement growth in Southeast Asia. His eyes grew large as he learned of the numbers of people who were being baptized each month. At that time, we were averaging about twenty thousand baptisms and starting over three thousand new house churches per month.

His brain swirled with what this might mean for the missionaries that his church supports. He dove into his questions, trying to understand what we were experiencing. He eventually asked the potent question: "What kind of seminary training are you providing for your pastors?"

I responded with, "Well, we don't have seminaries or ordained church leaders like you have in your church tradition. Movement leadership is developed in a different way."

I could see his confusion bubbling, but he had more questions: "What about discipleship curriculum? Since your leaders don't go to school, what kind of comprehensive biblical training manuals do you give them?"

> Movement leadership is developed in a different way.

I'm afraid that my next response only added to his confusion. "Our training is focused on our disciple-makers, often an oral learner who connects with someone in their household or in their house church who can read. We provide lessons that draw from the Word of God and applications in their own life and context. We don't have written products like you might buy from a denominational publisher," I added, "because we focus on providing easily reproducible lessons that reflect the realities of people in our world. Our people, primarily oral learners, are much the same as the peoples in the New Testament—not impacted as much by books or scrolls as much as life-on-life discipleship."

"What about church buildings?" he dropped in the middle of the conversation.

"We don't have any," I said, without explaining.

"Where do you celebrate the Lord's Supper, then?"

I replied that we do so in homes, when they meet as a church—again, just as was done in the New Testament.

"Who leads these house churches if you don't have any ordained pastors?" I could tell that his frustration was coming to a crescendo. I responded with a story about Aabad, who had recently given his life to Jesus, having had a dream in which a man came to him and told him to pay attention to what his friend Mahib was sharing with him about eternal life through Jesus Christ. He said that the man in the dream had holes in his hands.

After receiving Christ and being baptized, Aabad had led his family and five others in his village to Christ. He had started a 5-5-5 network (comprised of at least 155 people, which I will explain in chapter 8) and was leading a

What is a 5-5-5 Network?

Throughout this book, I will tell stories about people who have developed a 5-5-5 network. The details of how such a network operates will be fully explained in chapter 8. However, the basic system is easy to grasp. Here's how it works: One person shares the Gospel with a family member or friend, and when they find someone receptive to becoming a disciple of Jesus Christ, they baptize them. After baptism, the new believer is challenged to share his or her new faith with people in their social network until they personally baptize 5 people. This is the first 5. As he or she baptizes them, each of the 5 are challenged to do what was done with them and baptize 5 each, for a total of 25. This is the second 5.

Each of the 25 are then challenged to do the same and another 125 are baptized, for the third 5. This completes the 5-5-5 and a network is formed. As this organic method is worked out, house churches are formed with at least six baptized believers in each one, with 20-25 house churches in a 5-5-5 network. The person who started the network and helped coach and train each generation is considered the network leader and is the focus of training and teaching. They start Learning Communities of six to eight persons, usually comprised of the individuals house churches leaders who meet with them once a month to receive biblical and practical training to be passed along to the house church. There are about 155 people in each 5-5-5 network.

house church in his home, worshiping Jesus, and learning from the Word of God. Aabad was replicating what he had experienced in the home of Mahib, who had led him to Christ, focusing on obeying the teachings of Jesus and sharing communion in his house church.

My response to this American pastor's questions was almost more than he could bare. "Then what do our donations fund if you don't have church buildings, seminaries, or salaried pastors?"

I said, "Well, I don't actively do that type of fundraising because the organization of the churches is self-funding. We don't need Western funds for the maintenance of church life. Most donations that we seek are for the sake of training events, flood and food relief, and caring for the poorest of the poor."

> I don't want our churches dependent upon Western money, and I have learned that how you start is how you finish.

I continued, "I don't want our churches dependent upon Western money, and I have learned that how you start is how you finish. That is why the churches are self-funding from the beginning, and all pastoral care and teaching in the house churches are funded by the indigenous churches. We don't pay anyone for doing what Jesus taught us to do, and we have no church planters."

Why Movements Produce Fruit

For over two decades I have been paying attention to the inner workings of movement life, to look beyond the fruit to ascertain why movements grow as they do. In the mid-1960s, I committed my life to mission work, subsequently traveling the world, including twenty-five trips to Russia, and the former Soviet Union, and Eastern Europe, along with more than sixty mission trips all over China, Tibet, and Southeast Asia. I led teams twenty-five times to teach and equip pastors and leaders across South America, Cuba, Brazil, and the Amazon River region.

As I was training pastors and Christian leaders during this time, I began to pray about how my life and ministry efforts could have the greatest impact on where the largest number of people spend eternity. This prayer was my continual focus for many years, and the answer from the Lord served as the foundation for the work of this book.

The Spirit led me to conduct research around the question of what model of church would have the greatest impact on where the greatest number of people spend eternity. My initial research led me to conclude that the cell-church model has the most potential to have this kind of impact. Therefore, I began to analyze cell churches in twenty countries to determine the key drivers of growth, using both statistical models and qualitative assessment tools. Dr. Jim Egli and I were able to identify the key factors that result in conversion growth through small groups.[1]

Around the year 2000, I met Ying Kai in Hong Kong and heard about an extraordinary work that was producing tens of thousands of new converts every month in China.[2] Subsequently, my attention shifted from the cell-church strategy to understanding the dynamics of movements. I interviewed extensively and read all of the seminal thinkers in this space, including David Garrison, David Watson, and Curtis Sergeant, along with national leaders that I am not free to name here.

My wife Linda and I spent a week in Singapore, sitting in Bill Smith's International Mission Board training event for their missionaries who wanted to catalyze movements. I then studied and personally researched movements in Northern India, China, Southeast Asia, and Cuba, using the same analytical tools that I used in studying cell churches. I surveyed over five thousand house-church leaders, followed by qualitative interviews of movement leaders. From this academic-level research, and with the help of professionals in this space, we determined that seven root principles drive movement growth, which I detailed in my book *Movements That Move*. I will also introduce these principles in chapter 6 of this book.

> We are approaching 1.5 million baptized disciple-makers and well over 150,000 house churches.

After identifying these root principles, I felt led by the Lord in 2006 to initiate a pilot project to determine if what I learned through my research was functional and would produce a mass movement of disciples who make disciples. I began working with leaders in Southeast Asia, where the church's impact had been minimal, as less than 1 percent of the population identified as Christian.

This initial group of leaders that I began to train had about 250 house churches under their care, which has served as the seedbed for what has now surpassed even my grandest expectations. We are approaching 1.5 million baptized disciple-makers and well over 150,000 house churches.

---

1 This method of statistical research has served as the standard for many church research projects, including those reported in works like Schwarz, *Natural Church Development*.
2 Smith and Kai, *T4T*.

Counting the Fruit

The growth of the fruit within movements exceeds the expectations of even the most ambitious visionary leaders. In our work in Southeast Asia, we have seen more than three hundred thousand baptisms during the last year. This is the fruit of years of work. What began small has exploded in growth as we keep doing the work of investing in movement principles. Each of these networks began small, focusing on instilling the right DNA in the new converts; and as they multiplied disciples, the growth took off. In statistical analysis, this kind of growth is called a J-curve. In the initial stages the growth is flat and seemingly insignificant, but then at a specific point the growth shifts upward.

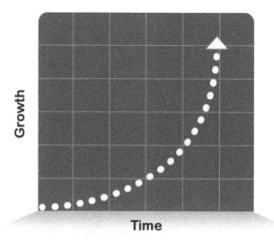

Jesus spoke to this kind of kingdom life in the parable of the mustard plant:

> What shall we say the kingdom of God is like, or what parable shall we use to describe it? It is like a mustard seed, which is the smallest of all seeds on earth. Yet when planted, it grows and becomes the largest of all garden plants, with such big branches that the birds can perch in its shade. (Mark 4:30–32)

God's kingdom work begins small and then it develops as its roots bore in the ground and its branches extend upward. No one would expect it to develop as it does because it begins so small. And if you examine any one church in a movement, it appears so simple. However, within that one church is the kingdom DNA that causes it to produce movement fruit and propels the mustard seed into massive growth.

The Fruit, the Roots, and the Branches

A common exercise in high school science classes is the black box experiment, in which the teacher sets up multiple sealed black boxes, each containing different items. Usually they include things like marbles, pencils, paper clips, and rocks. The students are instructed to identify the contents of these boxes without opening them.

In my early research work, my job was to identify the contents of the movement black box. One thing that has become clear in the research: focusing on producing the fruit itself does not result in movement growth. As soon as you fixate on the data or multiplication rates, you undermine your ability to produce the fruit.[3]

Consider an apple tree. An apple grower measures his success each year by counting apples, but he knows that the success of his harvest will depend on a variety of other factors. If he wants to reap a large harvest of apples, he must tend to the trees year around to make sure that they are ready to produce the fruit. The image of a tree helps us to understand how movements produce fruit, because there are roots and branches that are crucial to the life of a movement.

The roots grow deep to feed the tree that produces the fruit. Without these roots, it would not be nourished, and it would be tossed about by the winds and the rains and uprooted. The branches transfer what has been received in the roots to produce the fruit of that tree. The same is true of movements. There are trees that, because of their deep root systems, predate the life of Jesus on the earth and have survived all kinds of natural disasters. In one way, we could see the church universal as having survived and as continually thriving after two thousand years.

In *Movements That Move*, I identified the seven root principles that are crucial to movement life. These underlying factors that feed movement growth and give it stability are *All Lead, Immediate Obedience, Intentional Reproduction, Relational Discipleship, Passionate Prayer, Continual Training*, and *Strategic Networking*. We will explore these in more depth in chapter 6.

---

3 Goodhart's Law is relevant to this conversation. Charles Goodhart was an economist who stated, "Any observed statistical regularity will tend to collapse once pressure is placed upon it for control purposes." The British anthropologist Marilyn Strathern later boiled the law down even further: "When a measure becomes a target, it ceases to be a good measure." An oft-cited example of Goodhart's Law in action is the bounty on cobras that the British who ruled India supposedly paid to try to reduce the population of the snakes. Enterprising Indians quickly figured that they could earn money by raising cobras to kill and present for bounties. Goodhart, "Problems of Monetary Management," 116.

> The role of the system of branches is critical to the life and growth of both the tree and its fruit.

Movement branches are comprised of seven leadership practices that connect the root principles with the fruit. Again, to be clear, the role of the system of branches is critical to the life and growth of both the tree and its fruit. These seven branch practices, in combination with the seven root principles, provide insight into the essential components that advance movement fruit. This book presents a detailed look at these seven leadership practices.

The following pages expound on these roots and branches—the contents of the movement black box, if you will. However, before we unpack the roots and the branches that are discussed in the pages that follow, let's unpack a bit more about the fruit itself.

A Closer Look at the Fruit

In West Africa, a Western missionary had worked with a specific people group for over thirty years without seeing one church planted. Even though she had given her entire life to these people out of her love and compassion for them, she retired without leaving behind any sustaining fruit from her efforts. After her retirement and return to her home country of Canada, one indigenous Christian was trained in movement principles, and within a year he saw a network of twenty churches birthed.

This phenomenon goes by a variety of names, including church-planting movements, or CPMs; disciple-making movements, or DMMs; T4T (Training for Trainers) movements; gospel movements; multiplying house churches; viral churches; and simply "movements." The label of "church-planting movement" was first used to describe this unprecedented multiplication of churches in one of the first titles on this subject, *Church Planting Movements: How God Is Redeeming a Lost World*, by David Garrison.[4]

Since then, this phenomenon has been described and promoted through a wide array of publications and training venues that speak about the propagation and exponential multiplication of churches. A sampling of these titles include *Organic Churches*, by Neil Cole; *Viral Churches*, by Ed Stetzer; *A Wind in the House of Islam*, by David Garrison; *T4T*, by Ying Kai; *Contagious Disciple Making*, by David Watson; *The Kingdom Unleashed*, by Jerry Trousdale; *Movements That Change the World*, by Steve Addison; and my own *Movements That Move*. In addition, there has been a stirring within large, traditional Western churches that has caused leaders to embrace movement thinking, as seen in *From Megachurch to Multiplication*, by

---

4 Garrison, *Church Planting Movements*.

Chris Galanos; *Spent Matches*, by Roy Moran; and *Letters to the Church*, by Francis Chan.

These resources tell stories, make observations about characteristics of movements, and offer strategies for getting started down the path toward movement growth. They describe the reality of what is happening in the world today, which is the fulfillment of the hopes and dreams of missiologists and prophetic church leaders of the past. This is a manifestation of God's strategy for every local church to be self-governing, self-supporting, and self-propagating as indigenous manifestations of God's action—principles taught by nineteenth-century missionary thinkers like Henry Venn and Rufus Anderson.

Roland Allen, a missionary strategist from the early twentieth century, referred to what we are experiencing as the "spontaneous expansion of the church." This phenomenon is the realization of people groups coming to Christ through relationships within churches that fit their context, as promoted by Donald McGavran, who served in India in the mid-twentieth century.

The Fruit of the Chinese Movements

While I was attending a conference in Hong Kong, in 2000, I met Ying Kai, a church planter in China. He shared how his network of churches was seeing, in most months, an average of seven thousand new disciples made and three hundred to four hundred new churches. However, this kind of movement growth, while distinctive, is not an entirely new experience in the nation of China.

With the rise to power of the Communist Party and the rule of Chairman Mao Tse Tung in 1949, Western missionaries were escorted out of China. Communist rulers viewed Christianity as a Western religion that was foreign to their culture—a "tool of Western Imperialism," as their propaganda stated. At that point, there were only an estimated 623,000 Christians in the country, about one-tenth of 1 percent of the Chinese population.[5] Christian leaders assumed that with the closing of China, the gospel had hit an impassible roadblock.

However, when China reopened in 1979, the number of Christians tallied was shocking. Instead of a fledgling and stagnant group that needed outsiders to come in and restart the propagation of the gospel, statisticians reported an estimated 1.2 million Chinese Christians.

This provided the seedbed from which manifested growth that no one expected. Over the next two decades, it is estimated that about thirty-five million people gathered in networks of underground house churches

---

5 Xi, *Redeemed by Fire*, 8.

throughout the country, with another fifteen million who were members of officially recognized churches.[6] These numbers are disputed, as some think they are too conservative; yet even if we accept these minimal estimates, they are quite spectacular.

> The history of the Chinese church under Communist rule has revealed the unexpected phenomenon that no Western leader intended to produce.

These underground house churches are networked as movements that are advancing the gospel strategically and at great cost to their own lives. For the most part, they don't have physical headquarters, because such entities could easily be identified and destroyed by the government. They operate without foreign funding, as they are self-sustaining. They are self-governed by Chinese spiritual leaders who provide overall direction and training; but since close communication could lead to persecution, there is a great deal of autonomy in how ministry is conducted. In addition, they are not focused on maintenance. Instead, there is a great emphasis on sending out missionaries and reaching the lost, as they are practicing the principle of self-propagating, or what some call self-extending.[7]

Movement ideas are not novel missionary strategies developed by think tanks to get more converts and to raise more funds. The history of the Chinese church under Communist rule has revealed the unexpected phenomenon that no Western leader intended to produce. It developed under the radar, revealing a kingdom way of life that resulted in dynamic kingdom impact.

Ying Kai's father was a Baptist pastor in Taiwan, and Ying could have taken the established ways of church tradition with him when he became a missionary to China. Instead, he took a different approach. His network of churches is not based around his personality or strong leadership. In fact, one movement researcher put it this way, "I've interviewed church leaders in his network who don't even know his name or that he is the one who oversees their church."

Instead, there is a focus on a way of life that Ying Kai and his leaders foster that reproduces throughout the churches—a way of prayer and holiness. What God is doing in movements is not new, but it is taking off today in radically new ways.

---

6 "After the opening of China in 1979, Christianity made a startling comeback. By 2000, there were fifteen million registered Protestants along with five million members of the official Catholic Church. By some estimates, an additional thirty million Protestants and several million Catholics joined underground churches. Within five decades of the departure of Western missionaries, the Protestant population in China increased almost fiftyfold" (Xi, 205–6).

7 See Bach and Zhu, *Underground Church*, 257–68.

Defining the Fruit

When considering the fruit of Jesus movements, several key descriptions are crucial to understand.

First, a Jesus movement is comprised of people within a local context, and the way they organize themselves fits that local context. In the first modern-day book on movements, David Garrison wrote,

> A Church Planting Movement is a rapid multiplication of indigenous churches planting churches that sweep through a people group or population segment.[8]

Indigenous churches here means that the form of the churches is not imported from a foreign context. Missiologists have long argued that churches should not adopt the architecture or music styles of Western churches, citing examples of how early missionaries built in the tropics church buildings with high-pitched roofs, typical of churches built in Western Europe, or how they carried organs deep into Africa to play Western hymns.

> Movement churches are simple house churches consisting of at least six baptized believers and a recognized leader and are an integral part of a larger organization of similar churches.

Being an indigenous church, however, means refusing to import Western forms of church life. It means that the church form is simple and flexible, so that it fits the local context. In most cases, this entails some form of meeting as a small group in a home. I define it this way: Movement churches are simple house churches consisting of at least six baptized believers and a recognized leader and are an integral part of a larger organization of similar churches. These churches typically use music that puts Scripture to local, well-known tunes.

Second, a Jesus movement is led by indigenous leaders from the local context. David Watson, one of the earliest movement strategists, wrote that a

> Church-Planting Movement [is] an indigenously led Gospel-planting and obedience-based discipleship process that resulted in a minimum of one hundred new locally initiated and led churches, four generations deep, within three years.[9]

A movement is led by leaders within their context, not by outsiders. Foreign missionaries may initiate the movement and support it as partners, but the leaders are part of the local context, and they have the authority to guide how it grows.

---

8 Garrison, *Church Planting Movements*, 21.
9 Watson and Watson, *Contagious Disciple Making*, 4.

> They learn on the job how to do movement ministry, rather than being lifted out of their context to enter a program that will turn them into ministry professionals.

Third, these indigenous leaders are not gifted in spectacular ways, except by the gifts of the Holy Spirit, nor have they received training through typical ministerial training institutions. They are average Christians who have been released and empowered by the Word of God and the Spirit of God to lead within their context and who have been released by their mentors to lead. They learn on the job how to do movement ministry, rather than being lifted out of their context to enter a program that will turn them into ministry professionals, or even giving them credentials that others don't have and thus raising them above their brothers and sisters. Movements "turn average followers of Christ into [leaders] who invite their friends, neighbors, and workmates into small groups designed to hear from God through reading the Bible, obeying what He says, and sharing it with their social networks."[10]

Fourth, movements empower and train new believers to minister immediately after they are converted. Ying and Grace Kai use the word *training* because it is so foundational to their work. They not only train, but they also empower those whom they train to become trainers. They write,

> Church Planting Movements (CPMs) are the rapid multiplication of new churches that sweep through a people group or population. When we understand the ways and means of Church Planting Movements, we should begin training Christians immediately and make everyone we contact a trainer.[11]

Indigenous churches led by indigenous leaders foster movement growth and spontaneous expansion because everyone, even newly baptized believers, are trained. There is no waiting until people attain some form of maturity.

Sixth, people are trained through obedience-based discipleship. They experience spiritual transformation as they practice the faith in action, as opposed to entering an educational process that requires information. In his book *Miraculous Movements*, Jerry Trousdale states,

> In a nutshell, Disciple Making Movements spread the gospel by making disciples who learn to obey the Word of God and quickly make other disciples, who then repeat the process. This results in many new churches being planted, frequently in regions that were previously very hostile to Christianity.[12]

---

10 Moran, *Spent Matches*, 109.

11 Kai and Kai, *Training for Trainers*, 21.

12 Trousdale, *Miraculous Movements*, 16.

A crucial distinction is revealed here, which I will explore throughout this book. A Jesus movement is not really focused on planting churches. It focuses on making disciples; churches are a result of this. This discipleship is experience-based in nature, as people learn by doing as they experience interpersonal interaction and feedback. Many of the leaders within movements are oral learners who do not possess much knowledge about doctrinal issues. However, when they read Jesus's command to "turn the other cheek" or to "abide in me," they understand that obedience leads to personal experience of Christ and certain knowledge of his purpose and calling.

Finally, movements produce the fruit of multiplication as opposed to addition. Church observers and researchers often highlight churches that grow through addition as exceptional. They stand out because they add new members from year to year, growing by 10 to 30 percent. Recently, one of our large movements intentionally grew by 88 percent in one year, as the networks reproduced themselves during the year. Or they plant two or three churches on a regular basis.

In movements, there is "a rapid increase in the number of indigenous believers and churches that assume responsibility for planting other churches among the unreached."[13] At minimum, kingdom movements produce the fruit of "one hundred new locally initiated and led churches, four generations deep, within three years."[14]

> A Jesus movement is not really focused on planting churches. It focuses on making disciples; churches are a result of this.

The early stages of movement development resemble the lower flat leg of the J curve, as the new movement focuses on getting the DNA right. As they grow along the J curve, they are not growing through addition—i.e., increasing in membership by 10 percent per year and planting one or two churches per year. Such churches are replicating quickly and doing so at a rate that is blinding for many who have only experienced institutional forms of church life.

Sustaining Movement Fruit

During one of my research interviews with a missionary who served in the Far East, he told me about one of the first experimental movements that took off in a remote area of Southeast Asia. The results met all the common criteria of a movement listed above: Over one hundred people were led to Christ and

---

13 Global Frontier Missions, "Church Planting Movements (CPMs) and Disciple Making Movements (DMMs)."

14 Watson and Watson, *Contagious Disciple Making*, 4.

organized in churches led by people from the village, and it had multiplied to more than four generations. However, this missionary explained that there is not a single sign that this movement ever existed. They knew how to start a movement, but they didn't know what it meant to sustain it.

For the most part, the conversation in the movement space focuses on casting the vision for movements and how to begin one. These are crucial components, and they will be further examined throughout this book. However, the fact that Jesus movements are expanding like Jesus spoke of in regard to the mustard plant, we also need to explore how and why movements advance in a sustainable way over time.

> How do we go from four generations to forty and continue to expand and mature for decades to come, perhaps reaching four hundred generations or more?

Personally, it seems to me that we should be thinking about the systemic dynamics within a movement that promote movement life and growth over a period of forty years and beyond. How do we go from four generations to forty and continue to expand and mature for decades to come, perhaps reaching four hundred generations or more? In one of our movements, we have a leader who has started and completed forty networks himself, a total of over six thousand new believers, never receiving a dollar from outside the country. The institutional model of church would say we need seminaries and buildings, but is there another way to sustainability?

One answer to these questions is to consider more the nature of the roots and the branches that produce enduring movement fruit. In doing this, we may discover the essential values and practices that are necessary for both beginning and creating a movement that will last for many decades. God's kingdom life is contained in the smallest seed, the mustard seed; and when we understand the nature of that life and embrace it, we can join in what God is doing in the world and see movement life expand, as "it grows and becomes the largest of all garden plants, with such big branches that the birds can perch in its shade" (Mark 4:32).

Chapter 2

A New Testament Jesus Movement

Introduction

Many mornings I wake up and reflect on what we are experiencing in our movements in Southeast Asia and West Africa, and think, "We are living out the stories found in the book of Acts." I sit in wonder and awe at the fact that so many people are being transformed and that tens of thousands are counting the cost of becoming a disciple of Jesus Christ and a disciple-maker of others. Most endure some level of community or family persecution to join the kingdom of God and receive eternal life, yet tens of thousands respond positively to the offer of Jesus Christ. This is a unique time in human history, and it is truly an honor to be part of what the Spirit of God is doing in our world.

When I first started our work and implemented our research—the root principles that shape the way our movements grow and function—I had confidence that we were on the right track. I was focused on what our research taught us, and I employed the ideas, knowing that these practices agreed with the New Testament teachings. But I was also aware that some of the ideas conflicted with the way historical denominations were organized. Then, upon reflection, it became clear that there is a direct connection between Jesus movements we read about in the New Testament and those that are exploding around the world today. This chapter lays out these shared characteristics.

Rapid Growth

As I noted in the previous chapter, modern Jesus movements are experiencing nearly unfathomable growth. This has become such a part of everyday life that most of our people don't know what it's like to be part of a church that isn't growing like this. In the same way, the story told by Dr. Luke in the book of Acts demonstrates that growth was a regular part of their experience.

Some of the numerical references include:

- Acts 1:15—About 120 believers were meeting in the upper room
- Acts 2:41—About 3,000 were added to their number at Pentecost
- Acts 4:4—The number of men who believed grew to about 5,000
- Acts 5:14—A great number were added to their number
- Acts 6:1—The number of disciples was increasing
- Acts 6:7—The number of disciples in Jerusalem increased rapidly
- Acts 8:5–25—Many Samaritans believed "the good news of the kingdom of God"
- Acts 9:32–42—Many in and around Joppa believed due to Peter's ministry
- Acts 11:19–26—A great number of people in Syrian Antioch believed
- Acts 13:34–44—Many in Pisidian Antioch wanted to hear Paul preach
- Acts 14:20–21—Paul and Barnabas won a large number of disciples in Derbe
- Acts 16:5—Churches in Galatia grew in the faith and in numbers
- Acts 17:4—A large number of Jews and Greeks were persuaded in Thessalonica
- Acts 17:10–12—Many Jews in Berea believed, as did a number of Greeks

What started out as a seemingly failed messianic movement, led by one who was killed on a cross, multiplied through town after town without any mass communication strategies or the enforcement of those in positions of power. This organic infiltration passed through relationship networks and continued multiplying after the deaths of the first disciples until the early fourth century. Tertullian, a theologian from the third century, stated that Christians were as "a great multitude of men—almost the majority in every city."[1] While this claim was surely an exaggeration, it provides a general description of how the fruit of this kingdom movement appeared on the surface.

When one digs underneath the generalizations, we can fill in some numbers to understand how the growth of the early church developed. Rodney Stark, a renowned sociologist, applied his discipline to understand the growth of the early churches. He argues for a growth rate of about 40 percent per decade, which resulted in numbers along these lines:[2]

---

1 Kreider, *Patient Ferment*, 7.
2 Stark, *Rise of Christianity*.

Year	Number of Christians
40	1,000
50	1,400
100	7,530
150	40,496
200	1,171,336
300	6,299,832
350	33,882,008

Other church historians are far less conservative than Stark in their estimates, proposing that the numbers at the end of the first century were far higher. Missiologist Robert T. Glover writes, "On the basis of all the data available it has been estimated that by the close of the apostolic period the total number of Christian disciples had reached half a million."[3]

Whether one advocates for a high or low number at the early stages of the church's life, historians agree that the early church multiplied at an accelerating rate during the first three hundred years of its existence. However, the New Testament writings offer no language to suggest that the leaders fixated upon these numbers or made this kind of growth the goal; it was the natural outcome of the way that the church was formed. Just as an apple tree is designed to produce apples, so too the form of the early church was designed to produce Jesus-movement growth.

Where They Met

In modern movements, homes are the church's primary meeting place. Even with all the people who are part of our movements, we have not built any buildings. Likewise, the early churches met in homes. After Pentecost, they "broke bread in their homes" (Acts 2:46). As the church expanded through Jerusalem, they met "from house to house" (Acts 5:42). In Acts 12, we read about Peter being released from prison and thereafter going to "the house of Mary," where a house church was meeting for focused prayer for Peter. As Peter's ministry expanded into Samaria, he went to the house of Cornelius (Acts 10).

As the church expanded beyond Jerusalem and Samaria, houses continued to serve as the bases of operation. In Philippi, Lydia's house (Acts 16:14–15), along with the jailer's house (Acts 16:16–40), served as places where the churches met. In Thessalonica, it was Jason's house (Acts 17:5–9). In Corinth, the home of Crispus, a synagogue ruler, became a place of meeting.

---

3 As quoted in *Patzia, Emergence of the Church*, 142.

These are merely a few examples found in the book of Acts that lead us to conclude that homes were the central meeting place of the early church. This is confirmed in other writings as well, most overtly in Romans 16, where Paul sends greetings to the church that meets in the home of Priscilla and Aquilla. When they talked about meeting together as a church, they assumed that these meetings occurred in homes.

> Archaeology has uncovered no structure which can be both identified as a church and confidently dated earlier than a century or more beyond Paul.

In fact, we have no evidence that the early churches constructed special places for their gatherings. Eminent New Testament scholar James Dunn writes, "Archaeology has uncovered no structure which can be both identified as a church and confidently dated earlier than a century or more beyond Paul."[4] Their gatherings were woven into the norms of their daily lives, just as their faith was a part of their common lives.

The House as a Place for Family

Modern Jesus movements grow through relationship networks, and at the core of these networks are familial connections. Most of our house churches are comprised of two or three family units, as the gospel spreads both naturally and strategically as new converts share what Christ has done in them with their family members and friends.

In the early church, the role of the house was so significant that the relational structure of the home shaped how church members interacted with each other. They were more than members of an association. They were brothers and sisters, and such relations were facilitated by the environment where family is experienced. Roger Gehring writes in his book, *House Churches and Mission*: "The well-organized household became the model for a well-organized church. This is related to the fact that many house churches were small, close-knit groups with a nuclear family as their core."[5]

This began with the model that Jesus established in his three years of ministry.

> He [Jesus] chose "family" as the defining metaphor to describe His followers … one's family demanded the highest commitment of undivided loyalty, relational solidarity, and personal sacrifice of any social entity in Jesus' strong-group Mediterranean world. And the major life decisions were made in the context of the family.[6]

---

4 Dunn, *Beginning from Jerusalem*, 602.

5 Gehring, *House Church and Mission*, 298.

6 Hellerman, *When the Church Was a Family*, 31.

This model of interacting was more than a strategy for church life. It is a design built into the way that humans were created to live. In his book, *Paul's Idea of Community*, Robert Banks writes, "The comparison of the Christian community with a family must be regarded as the most significant metaphorical usage of all. For that reason it has pride of place in this discussion. More than any of the other images utilized by Paul, it reveals the essence of this thinking about community."[7]

The Size of Their House Churches

Our house churches are comprised of at least six baptized adults who are mature enough to understand and express faith in Christ. This is the case all over the world. And it was the case with the churches that met in the first century. Osiek and Balch note, "Comparing archaeological digs of houses at that time, a typical house might have fit comfortably between 6 and 15 people. If the crowd spilled over into the gardens, more could have gathered."[8]

Dunn adds,

> A church in such an oikos (usually translated "house") would consist of only a small group, of, say, up to twelve. Since "house" inevitably carries connotations of a larger property, such cell groups would probably be better referred to as "tenement churches."[9]

 Smaller groups generated space for storytelling, clarification, and interaction, and avoided one-way communication from a "knower" to a passive audience.

Such gatherings fostered dialogue and communal learning, which was common during this period. This stands in stark contrast to our modern-day assumptions, in which the primary content is offered as a monologue from an expert. Smaller groups generated space for storytelling, clarification, and interaction, and avoided one-way communication from a "knower" to a passive audience.

Even more, this setting provided a natural atmosphere for living out, or applying, their newfound faith to their common life. "Church" was done in an organic, life-on-life, pattern—one that could be easily replicated by anyone who experienced it. No special leaders with special training were required. House-church leaders were simply repeating the relationship experience that they had received as more house churches arose.

---

7 Banks, *Paul's Idea*, 49.

8 Osiek and Balch, *Families in the New Testament*, 30.

9 Dunn, *Beginning from Jerusalem*, 607.

Their Church Meetings

I will discuss how our house-church meetings work later, in chapter 10. Here I simply want to highlight the fact that they are highly interactive and participatory. Most New Testament scholars argue that this was also the case for the earliest churches. Banks states with an air of confrontation, "We find no suggestion that these meetings were conducted with the kind of solemnity and formality that surrounds most weekly Christian gatherings today."[10]

The two canonical letters Paul wrote to the church at Corinth provide the most insight into what occurred in church meetings. For instance, in 1 Corinthians 14:26 we read, "When you come together, each of you has a hymn, or a word of instruction, a revelation, a tongue or an interpretation. Everything must be done so that the church may be built up."

Paul says that *each* was contributing, as if what each member—not just the leaders—brought to their meetings was crucial to the life of the church. All were offering their words of instruction, sharing hymns, and exercising other spiritual gifts. Any preaching and teaching would have occurred in the midst of the ad hoc nature of the gathering. Through these relationships, the churches would have experienced worship, teaching, prayer, fellowship, evangelism, the Lord's Supper, and baptism.[11]

Leadership

Our leaders serve out of relationship and have authority because they are walking out their faith in active ways. This leadership is not primarily about putting people in positions and giving them titles to run an organization called "church." People are raised up as they have proven themselves to be servants. Leaders lead because they have produced the fruit of leading people to Christ and starting new house churches.

> Leadership was not a ministerial position or title as much as it was akin to the role of a spiritual father or mother.

As with most aspects of early church life, leadership was performed around relational—rather than formal—systems. The house (and family) provides a way of understanding how this leadership operated. One scholar uses the story of the church in Thessalonica as an illustration of how leadership would have naturally operated:

An example of how such a house-church might begin is given in Acts 17:1–9, where we read about the first Christians at Thessalonica who found in Jason's

---

10 Banks, *Church Comes Home*, 39.

11 Gehring, *House Church and Mission*, 27.

home a center for their assembling. The "head" of such a household would naturally be recognized as having oversight of the new church. His social standing would give him pre-eminence in the group; his close association with the apostle who founded the church and sought his assistance would add to this. And as time passed, the fact that he was the first (or one of the first) convert would further enhance his position in the group.[12]

It appears that Paul and other church leaders empowered those with homes who came to faith to lead churches that met in their homes. They did not send potential leaders away to school to learn how to serve the church. They rose up as they were mentored by others leaders and learned how to lead as they served.

Leadership was not a ministerial position or title as much as it was akin to the role of a spiritual father or mother. The leaders operated along the lines of the social structures of families where the churches met. New Testament scholar William Lane states, "The host who possessed the resources and initiative to invite the church into his or her home assumed major leadership responsibilities deriving from the patronage offered."[13]

Outreach

Modern movements naturally and organically expand through relational connections. Formal programs, promotional meetings, and recruitment efforts are foreign to our way of sharing the faith. In most villages, and even in large cities, where movements are expanding, growth occurs through natural social networks that are already established.

We see the same pattern in the New Testament, with three identifiable patterns. The first pattern developed as friends, family, fellow synagogue attenders, neighbors, and coworkers witnessed what God was doing in and through church members, and they would have observed what was transpiring in church gatherings. Regarding how outreach in the book of Acts was interwoven into the structure of a house and the shared meal, Rita Finger writes,

> What attracted people to the community? In a crowded city where most people lived marginal and often desperate lives, many cut off from previous kin-groups back on the land, Luke has truthfully portrayed what was probably one of the great attractions of the new movement: the inclusive and joyful daily communal meals held in the next courtyard.[14]

12 Giles, *Patterns of Ministry*, 31.
13 Clarke, *Serve the Community of the Church*, 164.
14 Finger, *Of Widows and Meals*, 244.

> The common life of a house was used as a way to share Christ with those in their network of relationships.

In other words, the common life of a house was used as a way to share Christ with those in their network of relationships. The way that the church met in the home was a testimony to what God had done in people's lives, and this would have been visible to those who lived nearby. This understanding of the book of Acts reminds me so much of my personal experiences in the house churches of Cuba.

The second pattern of evangelism, which involves a "Person of Peace," operated around natural relationships within the culture. The first person in a household who received Christ would serve as an inroad for sharing the gospel with that household and network of connections. A home would not merely consist of what we might consider a nuclear family today. It would be comprised of extended family members, slaves, and even those who worked together. The first convert in the house would offer a testimony about his or her experience with the household. A Person of Peace would have been one who had influence upon these people and therefore would have been a trusted means for sharing the gospel.

Michael Green comments,

The household proved the crucial medium for evangelism within natural groupings, whatever member of the family was first won to the faith. It was preferable, of course, if the father was converted first, for then he would bring over the whole family with him. This is what happened in the case of Cornelius when he contemplated a change of superstition. He gathered his blood relatives, his slaves and his friends, and together they heard the preaching of Peter. When Cornelius professed faith, his whole family (and it was a large one. When Peter entered the house "he found many persons gathered") was baptized with him. The action of the head of the family committed the rest of his dependent group. The same happened in the case of Lydia, a textile saleswoman from Thyatira operating for the time being in Philippi. Her whole household (no doubt largely slaves, together with some freedmen, but without spouse and children in this case, as she seems to have been unmarried) was baptized. So was that of the Philippian jailer when he professed faith. It was the natural thing.[15]

For missionaries like Paul, the house was the conduit for reaching people. Gehring concludes,

Householders were able to create an immediate audience for Paul by inviting their friends, relatives, and clientele. As a guest of the head of

---

15 Green, *Evangelism in the Early Church*, 210.

the household, Paul was automatically an insider and as such enjoyed the trust not only of the householder but of the entire household and everyone connected with it as well.[16]

The third way the house was used as an outreach base is more strategic and intentional in nature. A house in a city would serve as a base of missionary operations, through which people were sent to others in order to initiate new houses where the gospel could be shared. This is distinct from a centrally organized mission strategy, which was indicative of the church in Antioch, where the mother church sent out traveling missionaries who would report back regarding its results. Paul specifically appears to have moved away from that missionary approach to one where dispersed house churches became small bases to extend the gospel along organic networks.

The house church was not simply a way to attract people within a social network. It was a base of operation for sending out apostles into new areas. Paul worked through house churches, not through developing an organization of house churches for central control. Instead, the house churches became bases for developing leaders and teams to share the gospel in other unreached communities and cities.

Organic Networks

Most modern Jesus movements which have had any sustaining power and have continued to produce fruit have developed a way to connect leaders and churches as an organic network. This has been an emphasis of our work, which I will thoroughly explain in chapter 8 as I introduce the 5-5-5 system. In other words, the house churches do not operate independently. Instead, an organic order arises through networking.

In the New Testament, the word *ekklesia* primarily refers to individual gatherings of God's people in specific places.[17] The evidence does not point to anything like a universal church or a formal organization of churches. However, this does not mean that churches were not connected. This is made clear in Acts 15, where Paul presents his case for the inclusion of the Gentiles as part of God's people before the council at Jerusalem. These were not independent churches who were operating without connections to each other.

Networks operated informally, along relational lines. We see this through a variety of examples in the New Testament. For instance, Paul raised funds in many churches for the Christians who met in Jerusalem. There was a group

16 Gehring, *House Church and Mission*, 188.
17 Dunn, *Beginning from Jerusalem*, 599.

of leaders who traveled between the churches to encourage them, including Timothy, Titus, Tychicus, Onesimus, and Epaphras. The earliest and most faithful manuscripts of Paul's letter to the Ephesians actually includes no specific addressee; it may have been written as a circular letter to be passed between churches in different cities. Paul writes in many places of hearing reports about what was transpiring in specific churches.

Some form of organic networking evolved as the early churches developed. We see this in the way that Paul worked through churches as hubs to raise up apostles and sent them out to start new churches in new locations. We also see this as multiple churches met together in larger homes. However, it is difficult, if not impossible, to identify exactly how this networking operated.

In Albert-László Barabási's book *Linked: How Everything Is Connected to Everything Else and What It Means for Business, Science, and Everyday Life*, he uses complex networking to suggest that Paul was the master networker. His conclusions are not based on direct historical evidence, since we don't have such evidence at our disposal. However, his hypothesis is developed by reading between the lines of the available evidence and combining that with his research on how networks develop. He identifies four levels of a complex network:

1. Nodes. These are the smallest units of a network. In the case of a movement, this would be the house church itself.

2. Clusters. These are connections between nodes that possess a shared DNA. We might experience this kind of clustering when multiple churches come together or a leaders from multiple house churches join one another for prayer.

3. Hubs. At this level, the networking is more strategic in nature. A specific house church might serve as a primary avenue for sending out apostles or as a base for equipping. Is it possible that the house of Priscilla and Aquilla (see Romans 16:3–5) served as such a hub?

4. Complex organic organization. Here one might argue that Paul and his team served as an organizing team that connected the other three levels of the network.[18]

Again, we can only guess as to the specifics of how such a network operated. However, it is important to recognize that networks do not develop from a centralized institution. In fact, when hierarchical powers try to design such networks, that design will get in the way. The church of the New Testament developed, expanded, and was led along relational, organic lines.

---

18 Barabasi, *Linked*, 3–5, 7.

Conclusion

I have been part of a Western, institutionalized church in the Bible Belt for most of my life. I know from firsthand leadership experience how the church is "supposed" to work, and having experienced the Jesus Movement in America decades ago, I also intimately know the work of the Holy Spirit in our culture and churches.

Now, at the writing of this book, my eyes have been opened over the last twenty years to how the church can function in a culture that has no Christian witness. I am again living during a Jesus movement, but this time among Muslims and Hindus; and I am seeing the extraordinary work of the Spirit, much like in the book of Acts, but in greater scope and impact.

The stories of Acts are not merely a historical record about what the church once was. They are a preamble of what God is continuing to do today, as if we are adding new chapters to what Dr. Luke wrote almost two thousand years ago. He is the Lord of the times and seasons—and of history.

Chapter 3

Roland Allen: A Prophet of Modern Jesus Movements

Introduction

When I began working with house churches in Southeast Asia, I taught our key leaders about the seven root principles that had arisen out of my initial research of movements. When they embraced these principles, we started seeing a shift in growth almost immediately. House churches that had not seen any significant growth began seeing disciples baptizing new disciple-makers and seeing new churches being spawned on a regular basis.

Even with this, the introduction of these root principles was met with some misunderstanding and even resistance. For instance, a couple of our leaders gathered twenty to twenty-five recent converts and took them in a bus to the city to their brick-and-mortar church building. Then our ordained leaders baptized the new converts. They didn't understand that this traditional view of baptismal practice undermines movement growth. We worked with our new leaders not only to allow but to encourage new converts to personally baptize those whom they brought to Christ in their local setting and to encourage the new believers to do the same.

While these root principles were developed out of on-the-ground research within growing movements in multiple countries, my early leaders, some of whom were formally trained in traditional church orthodoxy, saw them as unusual. The practices we were focusing on challenged the status quo of how they had been taught to do church.

While our practices may seem new, they actually are not. They are built upon the shoulders of prophetic missionary thinkers who cast a vision of a new way of doing missionary work. William Carey sparked a wave of contextual missionary work that extends to this day as he used geographic and ethnographic data to identify people groups who had not heard the gospel.

Thomas Coke, the British Methodist who became the first Methodist bishop in America, stirred up Methodists to reach the world. Hudson Taylor, the founder of China Inland Mission, bucked the system and offended missionary leaders by wearing Chinese attire and speaking their language, even while in his own home. John Mott, winner of a Nobel Peace Prize, penned *The Evangelization of the World in This Generation*, a book title that also became a mantra for missions in the early twentieth century.

One missionary prophet in particular—Roland Allen—laid a theological and biblical foundation upon which movement principles are built. Of him, Lamin Sanneh, a missiologist from Ghana and a professor at Yale, wrote:

> Allen had set out to delineate the course of post-Western Christianity at a time when the church and his contemporaries thought almost exclusively in Christendom terms. That he did so with such undeviating consistency and unflagging commitment is testimony to his unique talents and Christian gifts. He was a voice crying in the wilderness, a prophet without honor in his own country.[1]

Allen wrote in the early twentieth century, but the fruit of what he taught—which he called the spontaneous expansion of the church—is just now being realized through the life of Jesus movements. His teachings are so significant because they identify key factors that form the basis of kingdom movements and provide a theological underpinning for the practical instructions that dominate the movement space.

A Prophetic Voice

Roland Allen, the son of an Anglican priest, was born in Bristol, England, in 1868. After attending Oxford, he followed in his father's steps and pursued ordination and attended a ministerial training school in the high-church Anglo-Catholic tradition. Soon thereafter Allen served as a missionary in China from 1897 until he was forced to leave in 1900 due to the Boxer Rebellion. Upon his return to England, he was married and had a child, and then went to China as a priest in charge of the local missionary station. However, he was only in China for a year, as an illness forced him to conclude his service as a missionary.

When Allen returned from China, he served as a priest in Buckinghamshire from 1903 to 1907, but he felt compelled to resign because of his convictions about the sacraments. He struggled with serving the elements to those who didn't show any evidence of the faith. It is significant to note that this was his last official position held within the church, as he thereafter served as voluntary clergy, earning his living through other means.

---

1 Sanneh, "Introductory Essay," III.

> My research has demonstrated that the demand that only ordained pastors perform baptisms and serve communion is one of the most significant limiting factors to the expansion of a movement.

The remainder of Allen's life was spent writing books and pamphlets and lecturing about missionary principles, challenging three basic themes: 1) established missionary methods; 2) the Church of England's acquiescence to secular law; and 3) sacramental churches' interpretation of the doctrine of apostolic succession. His writings on the first topic—including his classic, *Missionary Methods: St. Paul's or Ours?*—are directly related to the thesis of this book, although all three are connected when we read Allen's works within his own context.

His second theme relates to colonialism and the relationship between missions and the expansion of Western power and how this undermined the expansion of the gospel on the mission field.

The third theme pertains to the role of Christian leaders, specifically the demand that only an ordained priest or pastor can baptize and serve communion. My research has demonstrated that the demand that only ordained pastors perform baptisms and serve communion is one of the most significant limiting factors to the expansion of a movement. Allen saw this in the Scriptures, and he spent most of his professional life as a lay priest because he believed it to be faithful to God's ways.

About Allen, Lesslie Newbigin wrote, "He takes hold of you and refuses to let you go till you have admitted he is right. Whichever way you turn, he has an argument to silence you."[2] However, even with the wider exposure of Allen's writings decades after they were initially penned, far too often Allen is read through a lens that causes people to misunderstand what he wrote.

This kind of misreading occurs when readers search for techniques or formulas to make the church work. They examine a book like *Missionary Methods* for a strategy that they can fit within the current church system that will advance the church they know. As a result, Allen's ideas are adopted for a while, until the next good idea or trend comes along.

About this common way of reading Allen, Lesslie Newbigin observed,

I have heard of mission boards which decided to "apply" Allen's methods and proceeded to issue instructions to "the field" accordingly. The result could only be disaster. There are no "methods" here which will "work" if they are "applied."[3]

---

2 Allen, *Missionary Methods*, i.

3 Allen, ii.

Such readers might strive for spontaneous expansion, but they are trying to fit a set of ideas into an already established church system which sets boundaries that severely limit Jesus movement life. If we read Allen this way, it is impossible to interpret him rightly.

To properly read Allen's works, readers must be open to being shaped by a worldview that generates a way of being the church that aligns with what he calls spontaneous expansion. This requires a paradigm shift. A paradigm is a model, pattern, or way of thinking that serves as a grid through which we interpret ideas or phenomena. For instance, our experience in the established, institutional church acts as a paradigm which establishes a set of boundaries and rules about how church should or should not work. When we are exposed to teachings on church practices, we tend to fit those ideas into our established paradigm.

> Allen is not writing to lay out a few methods that can be adopted or tried out. Instead, he is summoning the church to submit to the work of the Spirit so that it can move along a new path for how to be the church.

Roland Allen's writings do not offer a set of methods or strategies that can fit into our established paradigm. Instead, they offer a new paradigm, thus requiring a shift in our imagination. Allen is not writing to lay out a few methods that can be adopted or tried out. Instead, he is summoning the church to submit to the work of the Spirit so that it can move along a new path for how to be the church. However, if one is stuck in what is often referred to as paradigm paralysis, a rigidity that hinders a person from seeing a different way of thinking, Allen's distinct way of thinking will not fit.

This observation about how Allen is offering a new paradigm and not simply a set of new ideas that can be fit into an old paradigm applies to the stance one takes when trying to understand how movements operate. Movement thinking and practice does not fit nicely within the thinking of the established way of being the church. It's like trying to mix oil with water. This is not a judgment of the institutional church. That's not my point here. If you want to understand how movements operate, you must understand them on their terms, according to a movement paradigm. Exploring Allen's prophetic words will help shape this paradigm.

Allen's Paradigm of Spontaneous Expansion

Allen was a high-church Anglican priest, who resigned his post and who was constantly challenging the common practice of mission stations where people within a local context were being asked to leave their culture and learn about Jesus within a Western outpost. He confronted the need for ordained clergy to serve the sacraments, when there were none for hundreds of miles and Christians were forced to wait for extended periods of time for a foreign church leader to come and do what they were not allowed to do.

Allen wrote against the Western control of finances in the mission setting. All of this he did for the promotion of the Spirit's work of the spontaneous expansion of the church, defining it this way:

> This then is what I mean by spontaneous expansion. I mean the expansion which follows the unexhorted and unorganized activity of individual members of the Church explaining to others the Gospel which they have found for themselves; I mean the expansion which follows the irresistible attraction of the Christian Church for men who see its ordered life, and are drawn to it by desire to discover the secret of a life which they instinctively desire to share; I mean also the expansion of the Church by the addition of new churches.[4]

Let's examine this definition within Allen's context. First, it entails "unexhorted and unorganized activity," a claim that might sound as if he is advocating for the absence of leadership or administration. However, within a church system, not unlike our own today, that is dominated by leadership and administration, where the church's activity is dictated from the center of the church's life where those in charge set the agenda for those who follow, he was advocating for a kind of activity that is fostered from within the lives of those of the church, those on the fringes. It is a kind of activity that arises out of the gifting and spontaneity of those who are doing the ministry, not those who are planning it for others.

It is the "activity of individual members of the Church," a claim that was absolutely radical for its time. When the church was set up for activity that was performed by the priest, pastor, or missionary, Allen is pronouncing the call for all to participate, as he advocates for a "priesthood of the laity" which would have entailed a serious adjustment of the job descriptions of the officers of the church. These "lay priests" would be involved in the "explaining to others the Gospel which they have found for themselves" as they are the people who are living in relationship with those who need to hear and see the gospel. They are living witnesses who demonstrate God's love as priests who connect the world to God.

It occurs as people see the "the irresistible attraction of the Christian Church for men who see its ordered life," through the activity of the actual participants of the church. The spontaneous expansion happens naturally

---

4 Allen, *Spontaneous Expansion*, 7.

because the inner life of the church is put on display as a beautiful, alluring beacon that draws the lost to it. It is not a chaotic, random life of individuals, but an ordered life shaped by God's Spirit. The lost are drawn to what they see "by desire to discover the secret of a life which they instinctively desire to share." It is not a movement of the gospel that is provoked through argumentation, manipulation, or guilt. They are drawn because they desire what they see, and they seek it because they desire to participate.

The result of such activity in the church is "the addition of new churches." From our perspective today, this claim to add churches seems obvious, but in Allen's context, we cannot avoid the paradigm-shifting connotation. This is not an addition of churches through the top-down administration of denominational headquarters, where funding and leadership is established at the center. It is the organic development of new churches by the people of God who have been stirred up by participating in this attractive activity.

Of course, our "attraction model" of church today is quite different than that of Allen's time. Releasing the "lay people" to be and do the work of the ministry includes missional sharing of the Good News and penetration of the culture with Christ's love and presence—an active role, not a passive, attractional model.

Allen's Rules of Practice

Roland Allen provided a new system that would guide leaders in how to establish an atmosphere where a movement can flourish, a hypothesis regarding the atmospheric conditions that promote movement life. This "atmosphere" is comprised of five elements that Allen observed in the missionary activity of the Apostle Paul.[5] He calls them "rules of practice" that establish a way of life that aligns with movement growth.

Accessible Teaching

Instead of developing teaching and discipleship that focuses on ordained pastors, the focus should lie on equipping the entire church to teach. All teaching must be understandable by and accessible to the entire people of God. The key—and prophetic component here—is "all teaching." Allen states,

> All teaching to be permanent must be intelligible and so capable of being grasped and understood that those who have once received it can retain it, use it, and hand it on. The test of all teaching is practice. Nothing should be taught which cannot be so grasped and used.[6]

5 Allen, *Missionary Methods*, 151–52.
6 Allen, 151.

We call this obedience-based discipleship. Disciples of Jesus put into practice his teachings and that of the other major teachings of the Bible. This was a direct confrontation of common church practices of Allen's time, when the sole focus was on the success of the pastor or priest of the local mission station. The activity of that vocational minister was the central focus. Allen wrote,

> In our day ... there has been a tendency to concentrate all functions in the fewest possible hands. The same man is priest and teacher and administrator, sometimes architect and builder as well. We have set up a purely artificial standard of learning as the necessary qualification for the ministry. We have required a long and expensive college education as a preparation even for the office of deacon. We have taken the youngest men and trained them to occupy the position of authority, such very limited authority as a native may exercise under the supervision of a foreign priest-in-charge.[7]

> This shift of the ministry focus is crucial for kingdom movements, as the ministry of the people cannot be viewed as simply an extension of the ministry of the primary pastor.

While some might argue that modern missionary strategies no longer use the mission-station approach, we are still haunted by it. The church system is set up for the sake of supporting and advancing the ministry of those at the center, not for the sake of equipping and supporting the people of God. This shift of the ministry focus is crucial for kingdom movements, as the ministry of the people cannot be viewed as simply an extension of the ministry of the primary pastor. The ministry of the people is movement ministry; it is the locus of the Spirit's work.

Simple Organization

The church, its leadership, and the oversight and care of God's people must be simple. The basic DNA of the way that the church operates must be basic enough that anyone can understand it, embrace it, and replicate it. Allen observes,

> All organization in like manner must be of such a character that it can be understood and maintained. It must be an organization of which the people see the necessity: it must be an organization which they can and will support. It must not be so elaborate or so costly that small and infant communities cannot supply the funds necessary for its maintenance. The test of all organizations is naturalness and permanence. Nothing should

---

7 Allen, 104.

be established as part of the ordinary church life of the people which they cannot understand and carry on.[8]

This is a challenge for most who have been part of the church for any length of time. As institutions age, complexity increases. It's part of the institutionalization process. Allen laments, "We cannot imagine any Christianity worthy of the name existing without the elaborate machinery which we have invented. We naturally expect our converts to adopt from us not only the essentials but accidentals."[9]

As a backdrop, the first thing we must say about Allen's paradigm is that his pursuit of simplicity—simple churches, simple leadership structures, simple teachings, and simple moral standards—is outstanding. In other words, he advocated for the elimination of Western superiority that placed unnecessary and complicated expectations upon converts. Allen wanted to see the people of churches empowered to lead and follow God in ways that fit their culture. About the work of the Apostle Paul, he wrote,

> Now if we look at the work of St. Paul, I think it must be perfectly clear that the local Churches of his foundation were essentially what we call native Churches. The little groups of Christians that he established in towns like Lystra or Derbe, Thessalonica or Beroea, were wholly composed of permanent residents in the country. They managed their own internal affairs under the leadership of their own officers, they administered their own sacraments, they controlled their own finances, and they propagated themselves, establishing in neighboring towns or villages Churches like themselves.[10]

Such churches can only be promoted if they do not have all the elaborate trappings of the institutional church and they meet in smaller, flexible groups without being bogged down by the affairs of managing property and buildings. "The Church expanded simply by organizing these little groups as they were converted, handing on to them the organization which she had received from her first founders."[11] The focus lies in freeing the "little groups" to discover how God is leading them to meet, without expectations that they will conform to the expectations that have been developed in another culture.

Local Leadership Control

As soon as we make a shift from institutional leadership practices to movement ministry practices, there is a corresponding shift in the control of the church

---

8   Allen, 151.

9   Allen, 6.

10 Payne, *Allen's Ministry of Expansion*, 10.

11 Allen, *Spontaneous Expansion*, 143.

organization. This is inherent in the hope for "spontaneous expansion." Allen challenges, "We can neither induce nor control spontaneous expansion whether we look on it as the work of the individual or of the Church, simply because it is spontaneous."[12] Movements expand at the fringes, at the edges, where new converts have life-on-life contact with friends and neighbors who don't know Christ. Movements don't expand at the center, where the leaders are doing the work of ministry.

> Movements expand at the fringes, at the edges, where new converts have life-on-life contact with friends and neighbors who don't know Christ.

This doesn't mean that there is no leadership or that there is a lack of organization. Leadership and organization are crucial. As a tree naturally grows at the tips with new branches, it does so because it is biologically organized to support that kind of growth. In the same way, movements occur because supporting systems are in place that align with that spontaneous life, but that life is not controlled.

> By spontaneous expansion I mean something which we cannot control. And if we cannot control it, we ought, as I think, to rejoice that we cannot control it. For if we cannot control it, it is because it is too great, not because it is too small for us. The great things of God are beyond our control. Therein lies a vast hope. Spontaneous expansion could fill the continents with the knowledge of Christ; our control cannot reach as far as that.[13]

There is no better test as to whether local leaders have control than to assess who manages the budget. Allen challenges,

> All financial arrangements made for the ordinary life and existence of the church should be such that the people themselves can and will control and manage their own business independently of any foreign subsidies. The management of all local funds should be entirely in the hands of the local church, which should raise and use their own funds for their own purposes that they may be neither pauperized nor dependent on the dictation of any foreign activity.[14]

Empowerment of the People of God

Ministry doesn't lie in the hands of a few. It is the work and privilege of all. It isn't enough to appoint local leaders who do all the ministry, as has been modeled for them by foreign missionaries trained in official schools. Allen proposes,

12 Allen, 12.

13 Allen, 13.

14 Allen, 42.

A sense of mutual responsibility of all the Christians one for another should be carefully inculcated and practiced. The whole community is responsible for the proper administration of baptism, ordination, and discipline.

> He speaks from his heart because he is too eager to be able to refrain from speaking. His subject has gripped him. He speaks what he knows and knows by experience.

Spontaneous expansion is fostered by the church members' personal experience of God. They aren't sharing Jesus with the lost because it's the right thing to do or because they have attended a class on evangelism training. Their experience of God's love motivates them to share what they know from that experience. Allen wrote about this in the third person, when we know he could have written in the first person: "He speaks from his heart because he is too eager to be able to refrain from speaking. His subject has gripped him. He speaks what he knows and knows by experience. The thrust which he imparts is his own truth."[15]

Allen observes that the experience of the early church involved miracles, which in turn illustrated that salvation had come and attracted the attention of unbelievers. Paul didn't plant churches by merely expositing the facts about Christ. He offered a demonstration of the kingdom that Jesus began.

> There can be no doubt that this power of working marvels, this striking demonstration of the authority of Jesus over evil spirits, was in the early Church considered to be a most valuable weapon with which to confute opponents and to convince the hesitating.[16]

This experience of God's presence and work by the Spirit overflows through people who comprise the church to the point that they want to give it away to others who have not experienced it.

The Ministry of the Spirit

The spontaneous expansion of the church is a work of the Spirit, not of organization. The Spirit equips and gifts the church—every individual—for movement expansion. Allen states,

> Authority to exercise spiritual gifts should be given freely and at once. Nothing should be withheld which may strengthen the life of the church, still less should anything be withheld which is necessary for its spiritual sustenance. The liberty to enjoy such gifts is not a privilege which may be withheld but a right which must be acknowledged. The test of preparedness to receive the authority is the capacity to receive the grace.[17]

---

15 Allen, 10.

16 Allen, *Missionary Methods*, 47.

17 Allen, *Spontaneous Expansion*, 144.

In his reflections on the church found in the book of Acts, Allen writes,

> It was the Holy Spirit who came to them with the fire of divine love. It was His presence which made them missionaries. Missionary zeal does not grow out of intellectual belief, nor out of theological arguments, but out of love. … But if this spirit is not present, a man is easily persuaded that to impart a knowledge of Christianity … is not necessary, nay, is superfluous expense of energy which might be better used in other ways.[18]

While there is much talk of the Holy Spirit in church circles and theological tomes today, Allen's time was devoid of such claims about the third person of the Trinity. He wrote in a time when the Trinity and the work of the Spirit was absent from seminary training and theological textbooks.

> That Spirit converts the natural instinct into a longing for the conversion of others which is indeed divine in its source and character.

The institutional forms of church life require new converts to align with established forms, reinforcing the advancement of the institution. New people are recruited to support the success of that institution and devote their energy to it. Institutional church life, which is based in intellectual Christianity, invites people to look to the center of the organization; but the Spirit stirs up love, a love that generates missionary zeal. Just as God is self-giving and outward looking, the presence of God by the Spirit causes the church to be likewise. Allen writes,

> The Spirit of Christ is a Spirit who longs for, and strives after, the salvation of the souls of men, and that Spirit dwells in them. That Spirit converts the natural instinct into a longing for the conversion of others which is indeed divine in its source and character.[19]

If the Spirit is alive in the church, then it will develop in its converts the character of God to see others come to know Christ. When the church depends upon intellectual knowledge, that missionary zeal will be absent.

Spontaneous Expansion and Jesus Movements

Allen's prophetic hope is no longer a dream or a theory one can read about in his books. It is a living reality. Many may examine modern movements in search for a method, a strategy that will produce quick fruit. They will try to boil movement life down to a formula that can be replicated and reproduced. If that is your goal in reading this book, you will miss the point altogether.

---

18 Allen, 9.
19 Allen, 9.

Instead, we must think in terms of establishing the leadership practices that promote kingdom movements. The five prophetic practices suggested by Roland Allen over a hundred years ago not only laid a foundation for the future of movements, but they also correlate with the seven leadership practices that have arisen out of my experience and research within modern movements. Proceed, as you read, with an openness to see what God is doing that can only fit within a new movement paradigm.

Chapter 4

Donald McGavran: A Father of Modern Movements

Introduction

When I was a young man, I had the privilege of taking summer missions classes, in 1965 and 1966, from Donald McGavran. After a long missionary career in India, McGavran was in the process of establishing the School of World Mission at Fuller Theological Seminary. His ideas were relatively new at the time, especially in American church circles. Little did I know that I was learning basic missiological principles from the man who would become the most significant missiologist of the twentieth century.

During his first five years of serving in India, his worked failed to produce one convert. The lack of results caused him to see the pride that many missionaries took in lifelong toil in the mission-station approach, although it often produced no fruit. Even more, he realized it to be a false pride that covered wasted lives and out-of-touch missionary methods that required nationals to turn away from their culture and embrace a Western, colonialist way of life in order to follow Christ.

I vividly remember listening to McGavran, a slight man with a moustache and goatee, piercing eyes, and a gentle smile, whose face lit up when he talked about Rolland Allen and the ideas behind the spontaneous expansion of the church. The balding gentleman with wire-rimmed glasses and a warm personality imprinted on my mind something that came to life thirty-five years later. After I had served in over fifty nations, equipping pastors and church leaders in various settings, from small groups to conferences with more than five thousand attendees, the Spirit led me back into the kind of research that Donald McGavran would have supported. I remembered his passion to see churches that were self-funding, self-feeding, and indigenously-led explode across the landscape. These three harbor lights that I learned from McGavran would guide me safely into the haven of seeing God develop an explosive movement that would reach over one million people with the transformative love of Jesus Christ.

While McGavran's missionary principles do not totally align with those found within movement thinking, they offer clarity about the movement paradigm and help us see how movements operate. Let's examine some of his central missiological teachings and examine how they relate to movement principles.

A Challenge to the Mission Station Strategy

The predominant mission strategy of McGavran's era was centered around a mission station, which would have been comprised of a school, a church, living quarters for missionaries, and possibly a medical facility. In his seminal book, *Bridges of God*, McGavran calls this the "gathered colony strategy," saying,

> Under the present strategy, Christian leaders tend to think of missions as a conglomerate mass of mixed chicken-raising, evangelism, medicine, loving service, educational illumination, and better farming, out of which, some time and somehow, a Christian civilization will arise![1]

A missionary would have been sent to establish or to run such a station so that lost people might be exposed to God's salvation. Commonly, when nationals became believers, they were extracted from their local context and invited into the station so that they could be discipled. They might even take on a job within the station, and as a result they would take on the social habits of the missionaries who ran the station. Therefore, Christianity was viewed as a Western religion that was irrelevant to daily life in the local context.

When McGavran observed the lack of results of established missionaries, he was challenging this basic strategy. He writes,

> Such mission work has produced not only extremely slow church growth, but also a philosophy of missions to suit. Conditioned by the slow growth, this philosophy has developed its own dicta of what constitutes "good missions," of how slowly the younger Churches must grow, of how permeation of non-Christian cultures was a good end as church establishment, and of how much philanthropy should be mixed with how much evangelism to insure a continuation of the mission in a non-Christian civilization.[2]

Missionaries assumed that this is the way missions should operate and that measurable growth should not be expected. McGavran observed that this

---

1 McGavran, *Bridges of God*, 103.
2 McGavran, "People Movement Point of View," in Pickett, *Church Growth and Group Conversion*, 3.

strategy raised many barriers to conversion growth so that any expectation for growth was unrealistic.

> The mission station was designed to offer a new social setting where Christ could be found, not to offer Christ within the context of an established social network in a manner that communicates his love in a powerful, effective way.

To become a Christian required people to leave their social setting, to cross cultural boundaries, and to uproot their sense of belonging. The mission station was designed to offer a new social setting where Christ could be found, not to offer Christ within the context of an established social network in a manner that communicates his love in a powerful, effective way. Converts, then, are to be extracted and re-socialized to fit into that institution in order to be "Christianized." Instead of experiencing the gospel within their context, they are required to re-locate themselves to be part of a church. This "gathered colony strategy" operates and is systemically structured as if the goal of Christianization is the building up of the institution, not the seeing and participating in the life and activity of God within the world.[3]

An Alternative Mission Strategy

McGavran proposed that the church expands through the social connections of people groups within local contexts. Growth occurs as the gospel is contextualized, thereby reducing cultural barriers that require non-Christians to cross unnecessary hurdles.

> Christianity ought to flow into every ethnic unit. Christ has commanded us to disciple to *ethne*—the ethnic units of the world. As Christianity flows into each unit in all six continents, it takes on much of its color. It becomes indigenous to that unit—that class, or caste, or tribe.[4]

In other words, the gospel spreads through shared social experiences in what McGavran called "homogeneous units." The homogeneous unit principle later became a hallmark principle of the Church Growth Movement, often being used to promote church strategies that seemed to advocate for racial division and isolation. This was not McGavran's point. He was simply making the observation that when a people group who have a shared-life experience embrace the gospel, the communication of the gospel with others in that people group flows naturally, thereby resulting in further conversions.

---

3 It is helpful to have a basic understanding of the history of missions in order to understand the root causes of the common missiological strategies. A classic text on this subject is Neill, *History of Christian Missions*.

4 McGavran, *Ethnic Realities*, 21.

"To Christianize a whole people," McGavran said, "the first thing not to do is to snatch individuals out of it into a different society. People become Christians where a Christ focused movement occurs within that society."[5] The gospel of Jesus translates into every culture, and any foreign culture that is attached to the gospel will only serve as a blockade to gospel communication. Evangelism and church growth occurs through the natural connections shared by people groups. McGavran explains,

> By "growing churches" we mean organized cells of the movement of a people. Folk join these cells by conversion without social dislocation, without entering a new marriage market, and without a sense that "we are leaving and betraying our kindred."[6]

Because the gospel expands along relationship lines within people groups, there are practical implications for how churches should operate. These implications correlate with later developments in Jesus movements.

Churches Are Guided by Indigenous Leaders

Central to original teachings on Church Growth is the promotion of indigenous leaders who would guide the church and serve as leaders. Even more, these leaders need not be highly educated, extensively trained, or monetarily compensated. Leaders who are connected relationally to those with whom they share life will have a greater capacity to communicate the gospel and equip the church, because they are part of the warp and the woof of the local context. As soon as social barriers are introduced—like requiring a nonindigenous leader to guide a local church—growth would be impeded.

Churches Are Organized into Cells

Practically, the church would grow by mobilizing people through social face-to-face gatherings so that members could minister to one another and open up their fellowship to others in their social networks who do not know Christ. McGavran writes,

> Small-group fellowship must be an evangelistic fellowship. Merely organizing small groups which have a warm spiritual time among themselves does not create growing churches. But if these groups are outward oriented, if they are concerned with the unchurched, if they win other members in the community where they live—in short, if they are evangelistic fellowships, then small groups are very important.[7]

---

5 McGavran, "People Movement Point of View," in Pickett, *Church Growth and Group Conversion*, 10.

6 McGavran, *Bridges of God*, 109.

7 McGavran and Arn, *How to Grow a Church*, 104.

These cells advance as part of the social connections—with family, neighbors, etc.—that are a natural part of their lives.

Evangelism Occurs through Average Christians, Especially New Believers

The work of evangelism is not the work of the paid, educated, professional leaders nor the purpose of church gatherings. In fact, gatherings are meant to equip and empower God's people for evangelistic work in their daily lives. Evangelism best occurs through the relationship networks of the people within the church. New believers have the greatest potential for sharing the gospel with the greatest number of people since they are still connected with people who do not know Christ. It is imperative, McGavran taught, to equip new believers to share their new faith immediately.

Conversions Often Occur in Groups

Because the gospel is spread along relational lines and because people groups (especially in group-oriented cultures outside the West) operate with a kind of "group mind," decisions for Christ often seem to occur in groups. Commenting in *Bridges of God*, McGavran wrote, "People groups become Christians as a wave of decisions for Christ sweeps through the group mind, involving many individual decisions but being far more than merely their sum. This may be called a chain reaction. Each decision sets off others and the sum total powerfully affects every individual."[8]

> New believers have the greatest potential for sharing the gospel with the greatest number of people since they are still connected with people who do not know Christ.

Many find this kind of conversion difficult to comprehend, especially if they have been shaped within an individualistic culture. It is often assumed that group conversion is not based in individual decisions for Christ. But A. L. Warnshuis argues,

> In group conversion, the individual is still as important as ever. Groups are influenced through individuals (parents or community leaders). The mistake occurs when the objective is only the individual who is separated from the group. Instead of separating him from the group, the individual should lead the way into the group.[9]

It is essential that the convert remain in contact with his or her group and influence them through their normal set of relational patterns.

---

8 McGavran, *Bridges of God*, 45.

9 A. L. Warnshuis, "Group Conversion," in Pickett, *Church Growth and Group Conversion*, 18.

The Importance of Research

McGavran based his Church Growth teaching upon the foundation of disciplined research, which occurred on multiple levels. First, he sought to understand the historical growth of a church, just as he identified the historical lack of growth in mission stations. He then would identify situations and experiences that influenced that growth trajectory over time. He observed that most churches and mission organizations live under a perpetual fog that hinders them from actually seeing the reality of their growth patterns. As a result, they don't even have a cause to ask questions about why they are or are not growing.[10]

Second, McGavran and his colleagues sought to understand dynamics that actually resulted in people coming to Christ and being added to the church. He wrote,

> The goal [of research] is through evaluation of the facts to understand the dynamics of church growth. Only as, on the basis of assured growth facts, we see the reasons for increase, the factors that God used to multiply his churches, and the conditions under which the church has spread or remained stationary, do we understand church growth.[11]

As a missionary, McGavran learned this from J. W. Pickett, a Methodist bishop in India who sought to understand the reasons why masses of people were converted.

> Far too many have promoted their understanding of why their churches have grown without doing the necessary research.

This kind of research sought to develop a deep understanding of why growth was occurring so that others could learn from it. McGavran argued that far too many have promoted their understanding of why their churches have grown without doing the necessary research, and therefore their reasoning is merely simplistic anecdotes.[12]

Third, McGavran's research incorporated the social sciences, including the disciplines of sociology and anthropology, in order to understand how

---

10 McGavran and Wagner, *Understanding Church Growth*, 54.

11 McGavran and Wagner, 92.

12 "Many American writers have told us why they thought their churches have grown. ... Yet until the particularity of church growth is seen, and until the many parts of the total picture are described one by one against graphs of the actual increases, there is great danger that the picture presented will be simplistic. Most of the reasons for church growth will not even be seen. A few will be overly emphasized" (McGavran and Wagner, 96).

different social groups respond to the gospel in different settings. This is illustrated by one of his final books, entitled *Ethnic Realities and the Church: Lessons from India*. He was in constant pursuit of a knowledge of how the church manifested in distinct social groups. This last area of research sets the stage for the next point of correlation between McGavran's themes and movement core essentials. Social science research is meant to provide an understanding of peoples, or ethnic groups.

Planning for Growth

> In other words, expectations that evangelism will just simply occur when people arrive at an ideal level of spirituality is an excuse for not doing the work of evangelism in the first place.

Growth through conversions does not occur simply because God wills it—as most assumed when McGavran was establishing his principles. Nor does conversion growth occur through some kind of romantic notion that it will naturally spill out through those who have been perfected. McGavran wrote in one of his last books,

Spontaneous evangelism, as one kind of evangelism practiced by super saints and filling all the rest of us mortals with joy as we behold it, is a very good thing. But when advocated as the only valid kind of evangelism, the chief kind of evangelism, or even the most effective kind of evangelism, it is dangerously close to being a sentimental, romantic structure whose real purpose is defensive.[13]

In other words, expectations that evangelism will just simply occur when people arrive at an ideal level of spirituality is an excuse for not doing the work of evangelism in the first place. Instead, McGavran taught that research must guide plans for church growth. For instance, research on people groups will reveal segments of society that God has prepared to hear the gospel. He writes,

The Christian who discerns those small segments of a total population which the Holy Spirit has turned responsive and who constructs a message about God's grace which is likely to appeal to those segments is likely to lead more lost sons and daughters back to their Father's house.[14]

Therefore, planning for church growth is, in part, a response to what God is already doing. Rather than trying to reach every group with equal effort,

---

13 McGavran, *Momentous Decisions in Missions Today*, 45.
14 McGavran, 49.

emphasis should be placed on those who are open to the gospel and therefore more likely to respond.

> Momentous decisions hinge on recognition of God's preparatory grace. As missionary societies become conscious of the human mosaic and study its many pieces, this doctrine calls them to focus attention on those ready to hear. They have become ready to hear not by accident, not by some fortuitous circumstance, but by preparation of grace.[15]

McGavran and the Movement Paradigm

This brief introduction to McGavran's teaching highlights core principles that correlate with movement thinking. First, Jesus movements not only stand in contrast to the mission-station strategy, but they are also distinct from today's common approach of what might be called the church-as-a-station strategy. With this paradigm of missions, a church is planted, a building constructed, and all the organizational trappings are developed in order to recruit people to extract themselves from their local context and enter into a re-socialization process as part of the church-as-a-station. The focus lies on developing and maintaining the organization of the church by recruiting people to join it and contribute to its continuation. Movements operate according to a different paradigm.

Second, as a contrast to this mission-station mentality, movements seek to reach people within their social groupings and empower them to lead people to Christ through their relationships without asking them to embrace a foreign way of life. McGavran highlighted the principles of indigenous leaders, grouping people into cells or house churches, empowering everyone to share Christ in their relational network, and the phenomenon of individuals within groups coming to Christ simultaneously—which are all central to movement life.

Third, McGavran emphasized disciplined research into what drives growth. However, this has not been a primary emphasis of those who have promoted movements to this point. The disciplined research has focused on describing the phenomenon of movements, as seen in the work of David Garrison. The thrust of my ministry over the last twenty five years has sought to apply McGavran's passion for research so that we might learn why movements operate as they do, asking what drives them and how we can empower people to lead them to reach the harvest fields of the world.

And finally, even more importantly, the fourth point is that this research should lead to planning that will produce movement fruit. As we better

---

15 McGavran, 50.

understand movement dynamics, including why and how they happen, we can be effective in participating in what God is doing through them.

Conclusion

McGavran did not develop a movement strategy, nor did he ever come close to observing or studying anything like we are seeing today. However, he was a pioneering thinker who broke the mold of the old mission station, colonial approach and established foundational missiological principles on which movement thinking could be built.

Chapter 5

Understanding How Movements Work

Introduction

When I wrote my book *Movements That Move* in 2015, it was one of the few books available at the time that attempted to explain what was going on in Jesus movements. Today that has changed. Many are waking up to what God is doing, and they want to lead the church in this direction. Resources—both books and online—are available to equip leaders.

In the book *Bhojpuri Breakthrough*, we read about a movement in northern India which began in the mid-1990s. The number of disciples and house churches are so vast that Victor John and other leaders are not able to track the viral expansion of disciples who are making disciples. And this movement has flourished in a region of India that was judged to be a "graveyard of missions."[1] Or consider the more academic-style analysis found in the book *Motus Dei: The Movement of God to Disciple the Nations*, where we can read a variety of articles that are steeped in both theological and phenomenological research.[2]

Some large churches in North America have concluded that their traditional efforts, even though they proved successful by common standards, are not actually effective enough. For example, the leadership of Experience Life Church in Lubbock, Texas, began to ask what it would take for them to reach one million people in the next ten years. Based on their previous growth rate, it had cost them about five thousand dollars per convert to grow to their highest size. They did the math and determined that doing church in a way that would cost five billion dollars to reach one million people would not be acceptable. Therefore they had to make a shift in their strategy and adopt movement principles. We read about this shift in the book *From Megachurch to Multiplication: A Church's Journey toward Movement*.

1 John with Coles, *Bhojpuri Breakthrough*.
2 Farah, *Motus Dei*.

Or consider the words of Francis Chan in his book *Letters to the Church*. There he outlines his personal journey away from leading a large, successful megachurch to facilitating a growing network of small, simple churches. He felt led to change his approach only in part because of the data. Even more, his primary motivation, like that found in the writings of Roland Allen, came from his rereading of the New Testament experience of the church. Chan writes,

> The Church was meant to be a beautiful army, sent out to shed light throughout the earth. Rather than hiding together in a bunker, we were supposed to fearlessly take His message to the most remote places. People should be in awe when they see His people with a peace that surpasses comprehension and rejoicing with inexpressible joy (Phil. 4:7; 1 Pet. 1:8). … Have people ever been in disbelief over the amount of peace you display? Are you known for being ridiculously joyful? Add that to "the immeasurable greatness of his power in you" (Eph. 1:19) and you cannot go unnoticed. We have tried to attract people through so many different strategies. What if they saw an army of people with inexpressible joy, peace that surpasses comprehension, and immeasurable greatness of his power? How could they not be intrigued?[3]

> Only those who go beyond seeing the paradigm and take the next step of developing systems that produce movement fruit will reap the harvest of a movement.

It is truly exciting to see the growing interest and enthusiasm regarding movements. The vision is bubbling up. What was once happening beneath the surface is becoming a reality that cannot be ignored. It is not enough, however, merely to look at the data and jump on the bandwagon of excitement. Many want the fruit. They want to see the church have this kind of impact, but only those who go beyond seeing the paradigm and take the next step of developing systems that produce movement fruit will reap the harvest of a movement. In other words, the focus does not lie on producing the fruit. Movements move because they are designed in such a way to foster a specific way of life that results in the fruit. There is a specific movement DNA, an organizational system, that creates an environment where movement growth can be realized.

There are many who have invested extensively in the promotion of the movement vision, seeking to shift the momentum of missions to movement thinking. We are getting there. Many mission agencies, churches, and church networks are more ready than ever to try their hand at catalyzing movements.

---

3 Chan, *Letters to the Church*, 18.

As a result, there are thousands of start-up movements. By start-up, I mean there are four generations of growth in four unique streams of people. These young movements could benefit from investing in the hidden DNA that will produce long-term, sustainable fruit. If the catalyzer is patient and acts with foresight and wisdom, then a movement may be ignited that will produce the amazing fruitfulness of the New Testament work of the Apostle Paul. It is like starting a small fire with a bit of tinder and a match. It may require patiently blowing on the fire and allowing the tinder to catch fire before adding the right size of kindling to take the fire to the next level. Movements that produce sustaining and growing fruit are founded on systems that support the new converts in reaching their social networks. Without these systems of support, the fire can easily die.

Thinking about the Church as a System

Every group of people who works together over time form a system to sustain their way of operating and reaching their goals. These systems may be either articulated or unspoken social contracts that define how the group will work together to accomplish their goals. To maximize their effectiveness in reaching their goals, all social groups need to develop systems. These range from the rules of backyard football to the rules of the military—perhaps the greatest example of a top-down system of command and control. Although the military is not an appropriate model for movements, it is a great example of systems development. In our world today there are many examples of complex church systems, built around the idea that their traditions and systems are the ones everyone should follow.

Probably the greatest challenge to reaching lost people today is that churches may say their primary purpose is to preach the gospel around the world, but when we look below the surface we see systems that are designed to replicate their doctrines and practices and duplicate exact replicas of themselves. This is common, but when we look below the surface we see systems that are designed to replicate exact duplicates of the current practices. In fact, we could visit churches of almost any denominational body in multiple cultural settings, and if the language was one we understood, we would feel right at home, because the meetings are conducted exactly like those from the sending churches. Systems always reproduce themselves, unless there is a specific and focused strategy to start new systems. This is the default of almost all church bodies. When they fail to be easily identifiable as springing from the parent church, then it is likely that the sending church body will pull their support.

> Efforts to create massive movements may be frustrated if we don't dig deeply and think about every component in our system.

Thus, we have the conundrum. Organized church bodies who want to reproduce their systems, often with just a tweak in style or a language change, in hopes of seeing mass movements to Christ, fail to recognize the deep change required to be successful. Deep change is never easy, whether for an individual or a group of people. It requires facing our fears and our need for control and putting our traditions on the altar for God's fire to fall on. When our systems, built for one culture and tradition, are shoehorned into a movement effort, then something must give. Given enough freedom, the new efforts may blossom and bloom; but if the resulting new life doesn't have enough of the parent organization's systems to easily identify it as a child, then conflict may follow. Most likely the blossoms will not flower and reproduce a movement because there will be built-in systems that are in conflict with movement growth values and best practices. Perhaps we need to take a deeper look at movement-system paradigms and identify the critical components that enable and empower new life that is reproducible in most contexts.

Often when we see the paradigm of Jesus movements, we fail to see how the output of movement life calls for a totally different kind of system. Instead, we try to add a few movement strategies to their already established system and hope that we will get movement results. But systems don't work this way, because they cannot be broken into parts. The Oxford English Dictionary states that a system is "a set of things working together as part of a mechanism or interconnecting network." The system that works is comprised of parts, not a list of parts that can be put together to make a whole. These parts work together to make the whole because they are interconnected in a specific way to produce a specific outcome.

Systems expert Daniel Kim writes, "In the most basic sense, a system is any group of interacting, interrelated, or interdependent parts that form a complex and unified whole that has a specific purpose. The key thing to remember is that all the parts are interrelated and interdependent in some way."[4] Therefore, the introduction of a new part, no matter how revolutionary it might be, will not have a revolutionary impact upon the output of an organization unless the entire system is redesigned to fit the new "specific purpose." We have all seen this challenge play out in our families, businesses, or churches when we hear about the latest, greatest idea that will change everything, and we try it—only to be disappointed, looking for the next new trend.

---

4 Kim, "Introduction to Systems Thinking," 2.

Efforts to create massive movements may be frustrated if we don't dig deeply and think about every component in our system. What needs to go, what needs to be modified, and how painful will the changes be? How clear are we about what we want to see happen, and are we willing to "count the cost" to our existing system? We must see the system as a whole, and look at how we will recognize what the Spirit of God is doing, and cooperate with him. Working in a totally different culture, how will we develop a new system, and what will that look like when it's functional?

Understanding a Movement System

Consider the success of the University of Alabama football team. One might analyze the winning record and the multiple national championships in order to understand what is going on. This makes for splashy headlines, but it will not reveal why this program has been so successful. You could go a bit deeper and examine the in-game decision making or the specific game plans developed by Coach Nick Saban and his staff to defeat their specific opponents on any given game day. However, this insight will only point to a specific tactic or strategy adopted for that game or for that season. This will not provide insight into the ongoing success of the program because if you look at Saban's career, he has changed his strategies year after year.

> If you want to see the fruit of Jesus movements, you must look beneath the surface of the fruit and go beyond identifying specific tactics or strategies.

We must look deeper. The key to Saban's success as a coach has more to do with what happens outside of the games, what he calls "The Process." It is based on the patterns of behavior and the underlying infrastructure that he has built to support the actions and events. Because Nick Saban has learned that achievement is only possible with focused effort in the present moment, he insists that his players, assistant coaches, and himself give all of their energy to the here and now. The legendary coach tells us: "Becoming a champion is not an easy process. It is done by focusing on what it takes to get there and not on getting there."[5] All of this occurs beneath the surface.

If you want to see the fruit of Jesus movements, you must look beneath the surface of the fruit and go beyond identifying specific tactics or strategies. You must look at the underlying, hidden system or infrastructure that is designed to produce and support the fruit. Think of a movement system as having the four parts of a tree: the fruit, the leaves, the roots, and the branches.

5 Saban and Curtis, *How Good Do You Want To Be?*, 3.

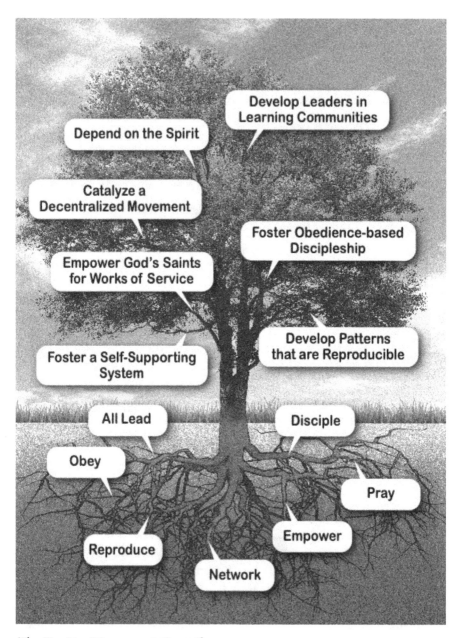

The Fruit—Movement Growth

The output of changed lives, massive numbers of new converts, and the multiplication of simple churches is the most visible aspect of movements, and it has garnered a lot of attention in the form of statistical reporting and testimonial stories, both of which produce a great deal of excitement. Many resources focus a great deal of attention at this level, sharing stories about lives that have changed, about leaders who have risen up to lead thousands, and about how neighborhoods have been transformed. This is equivalent to looking at the scoreboard to see who is winning the game.

The Leaves—Movement Traits

The visible phenomena of movements are strategic in nature as they can be described by simply observing the common characteristics. While specific nuances vary between different movements around the world, there are common elements. Victor John identified the following:

- Passionate Prayer
- Instantaneous Personal Witnessing
- A Culture of Empowerment
- Reaching Friends and Relatives
- The Word Is the Foundation
- Intentional Planting and Reproduction
- Obedience and Accountability to the Word
- Cultural Relevance and Holistic Service
- Sensitivity Toward Other Religions
- Partnership[6]

Neil Cole developed his own list of traits in his book, *Church 3.0: Upgrades for the Future of the Church*, as follows:

- Decentralized: no central control center must approve all decisions. Everyone is empowered with the work so that the movement spreads to the outskirts spontaneously without needing permission or support.
- Composed of self-replicating units of people at every level of development—disciples, leaders, churches, and even movements themselves. Every unit of church life must be capable of reproducing itself without needing persuasion, manipulation, or programs from the outside.
- Minimal organizational structure that is dictated by the life of the church, not the other way around. We say, "Don't organize it until you have an it to organize … and even then, go slow."
- Does not depend on outside resources. All resources for the harvest are found in the harvest. Part of what a CPM does is redeem what was stolen from God by the Enemy. All that is necessary for a harvest can be found in the harvest.

---

6 John with Coles, *Bhojpuri Breakthrough*, 171–85.

- Driven by ordinary Christians who have been transformed by God and who cannot help but share the Good News. Absolutely essential, this is the fuel of the spreading movement.

- Relationally linked rather than corporately or organizationally bound. It is not an accepted application and dues that hold these churches together, but relationships. They are not bound in dependence on one another; nor are they independent—they are interdependent.

- Characterized by reproduction at all levels simultaneously. This reproduction develops first in the smallest unit of church life and then spreads throughout, ultimately reaching the global scope of a movement.

- Begins its momentum with the spiritual, before the strategic.

- Moves evangelism from individual conversions to group conversions. Entire households, social webs, and tribes come to Christ rather than individuals.

- Dedicated to having kingdom life touch the domains of society and culture, not just individual lives. The people of such a movement represent Christ's kingdom incarnationally throughout all parts of society.[7]

I include both of these lists because they describe the external forms, the visible patterns that are common to movements. They help us understand what the system looks like on the surface, but there is more that lies beneath the visible attributes.

The Roots—Movement Principles

In *Movements That Move*, I wrote about seven root principles that drive movement strategies and produce movement fruit. These principles were identified through extensive qualitative interviews of movement strategists and movement practitioners, as well as quantitative statistical research and modeling, using surveys of more than five thousand house-church leaders in China, India, Bangladesh, and Cuba. These principles name the underlying patterns within movement systems that have an ongoing impact. They are:

1. All Lead. The leadership of simple churches is not limited to those who have special training or have been officially ordained. In fact, all are empowered to baptize and all are released to serve communion. As soon as limits are placed on who can and cannot lead, movements wain.

2. Immediate Obedience. People in movements grow by doing, not by sitting in a classroom. The common description in movement literature

---

7 Cole, *Church* 3.0, 84.

calls this obedience-based discipleship. The crucial aspect is that obedience is sparked immediately after a person becomes a Christian. They don't wait until they grow to a predetermined level to obey. They are challenged to learn and act, and a major action is sharing their faith. Since they are new Christians, they are taught how to tell family and friends about Jesus's love without taking them out of their context. They learn to obey within their relationship network without having to be extracted from it.

3. Intentional Reproduction. Movement fruit depends upon reproduction. This means that every aspect of movement life must be developed so that all can reproduce it. If a missionary imports an approach from a Western setting that depends upon his expertise, then it is not reproducible. It must be designed to fit the context of the local people, not the expectations set by a foreign culture. The goal is for all to reproduce, to give what God has given to them, and to begin doing so immediately after they have given their life to Christ. Every activity must be modeled so that it can be replicated in the same way. If a house-church leader in a village cannot reproduce the experience, then it must be designed so that he can receive and reproduce it and thus pass it on to others who will do likewise.

4. Relational Discipleship. Immature Christians grow through life-on-life interaction, not through classroom information saturation. Mentoring in a community is the key, not the dispersal of concepts about theological claims. This does not mean that theology is not important or that God's truth vacillates within movements. The Bible is central, but people learn the truth of the Bible as they walk together, not in isolation.

5. Passionate Prayer. Movement prayer is not perfunctory or ritualistic. People don't pray because it's the right thing to do. They pray because they are drawn by the experience of the living God by the Spirit. They pray because they are experiencing persecution. They pray because they have faith for a miracle because they have previously been the recipient of a miracle.

6. Continual Training. Ongoing movement growth advances because there is a natural and organic process for people to learn and grow together continually, even after they have been discipled. Arriving at a plateau and becoming a spectator Christian is not part of movement life. Perpetual equipping is built into the system, as truth passes from leader to leader and down through the house churches.

7. Strategic Networking. The gospel is proclaimed strategically through the recognition of apostolic leaders who are gifted to spark pockets of movements in new relational networks. This is done primarily by identifying "persons of peace" (based on Luke 10) who are open to the gospel and have an influence upon a social group.

The next chapter goes into more depth about each of these seven root principles, providing insight into the research that lies behind them.

The Branches—Movement Leadership Practices

The fruit develops through the life that flows through the branches of the tree. The branches must be designed not only to produce that fruit, but also to support and sustain it. Branches provide this function because they connect the nutrition that is drawn through the roots with the fruit. In a kingdom movement, the life that is produced through the root principles flows through the branches of the leadership practices to produce the fruit. These seven practices are introduced in chapters 7 through 13.

> In a kingdom movement, the life that is produced through the root principles flows through the branches of the leadership practices to produce the fruit.

The seven root principles are the infrastructure of a movement, providing the dynamics of growth that cause the unencumbered growth. These may be hidden to most everyone looking for the reasons for massive growth. Roots are typically underground and hidden. For example, the leadership principle of lay people baptizing is really a root principle that addresses what it means to lead and who is qualified to actually do the work of ministry.

The seven leadership practices are the observable "branches" on which the fruit hangs, using that metaphor. These practices bring the principles to life. They are critical to the production of leadership and Spirit-empowered people. They support the whole by providing long-term financial independence and patterns of equipping that are fully reproducible at the local level.

Conclusion

All four parts of the tree are important to the systems of the tree. If a farmer only observes the fruit during harvest season, he will fail to understand which farming practices produce the best fruit. Likewise, we need to dig deeper than just looking at the outward results, but also focus on the root systems and the best practices that are vital parts of the systems that are driving the fruit production.

Chapter 6

The Root Principles

During the 1990s I was traveling the world, training national church leaders and pastors in the art of prayer and basic church-development principles. While doing so I had the opportunity to do qualitative and quantitative international research on the conversion-growth dynamics that were driving small-group growth and multiplication of the well-known small-group churches of the day. Through the discipline called "predictive analytics," our team was able to identify key factors that resulted in the conversions of individuals via small groups and the resulting group growth as people became disciples of Jesus Christ. This discipline employs data and statistical analysis to identity the underlying, hidden factors so that we might be able to understand future results if certain practices are adopted. In other words, we identify the causes that produce specific results from statistical analysis in order to predict what is more likely to occur when we invest in those causes.[1]

> We identify the causes that produce specific results from statistical analysis in order to identify what is more likely to occur when we invest in those causes.

In the year 2000, upon learning about the massive Jesus movements in China through meeting Ying Kai in Hong Kong, I used that same analytical approach to study what drives movement growth. We began the process with qualitative analysis, interviewing key missionary leaders who were promoting the paradigm worldwide, as well as national practitioners who were working within existing movements of the day. From this deep dive into face-to-face interviews in various parts of the world, including a visit to Bill Smith's training of the IMB's missionary force in Singapore, we developed the best practices that

---

1 This form of research has been employed by many, including that found in Schwarz, *Natural Church Development*; Hawkins and Parkinson, *REVEAL*; Stetzer and Rainer, *Transformational Church*.

seemed to be commonly taught and followed, integrating them into an extensive survey of more than a hundred questions.

Then we asked more than five thousand house-church leaders within movements in India, China, Cuba, and Southeast Asia to complete these surveys. This data was analyzed in three iterations to determine the factors that impacted the dependent variables, which were numbers of baptisms and new house churches. The goal of all this research was to find the independent variables, or root principles, that were affecting the outcomes of conversion growth and church multiplication.

Seven factors stood out as having significant impact on the results we wanted to achieve—the fulfillment of the Great Commission. In other words, the statistical analysis revealed that these seven factors, when properly contextualized in the culture in which we are working, will empower movement growth. As a side note, I will mention that most of this work was completed by 2010. Around 2015, a model of movement growth called Disciple Making Movements, or DMM, became popular. Our research revealed many of the same best practices as the DMM model, and in 2011 the Holy Spirit gave us a multigenerational approach—called 5-5-5—that provided extra fuel to these ideas.

One difference between many DMM models and our 5-5-5 model is the DMM emphasis on using the Discovery Bible Study method of outreach. Although effective, we don't use this approach as an evangelistic tool. Proclamation of Christ in a culturally appropriate manner within a social network is our preferred approach to sharing the message of Christ.

> Without a coherent system, massive and sustainable growth is virtually impossible to sustain.

I wrote about these seven root principles in *Movements That Move*. The following provides a brief introduction to them, along with a simple analysis of some high points of the data. It's important to note that the leadership practices found in subsequent chapters are directly connected to these root principles. The leadership practices are tangible ways that these root principles are put into motion within a movement. As stated previously, and I cannot overemphasize this point, these root factors and best leadership practices work together as part of a system, with the leadership practices acting as the branches that extend up from the roots. Without a coherent system, massive and sustainable growth is virtually impossible to sustain.

Root Principle #1 Simple Leadership

Our research has revealed that Jesus movements are propelled by a different kind of leadership. Rather than depending upon specialized roles that require unique leaders, movements thrive with "simple" leadership, which means, potentially, that everyone can participate as a leader. No one is excluded from the opportunity to lead others. Movement leadership is stripped down to its most basic level so that anyone can lead others into life with Jesus. To be clear, our model encourages new converts to share their faith with others, perform baptisms for those they bring to faith in Christ, lead their house churches, and lead in sharing communion. In every case disciples are being mentored, but there are no classes or series of benchmarks that they must perform before being empowered to lead in these basic areas.

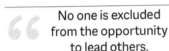
> No one is excluded from the opportunity to lead others.

Simple leadership is fostered through the roles that the house-church believers play, and—critical to note—the new converts see a model where everyone is leading. In most oral societies, leadership roles are reserved for the educated; yet in the 5-5-5 church life, oral learners are seeing their own lead. The significant impact of this reality is difficult to measure.

Also, for the Western mind, this is where the institutional model of church and the New Testament model come into conflict in a very real way on many different levels: the "attraction" approach and the "movement" approach butt heads. In the attractional pattern of doing church, there is usually an identifiable church building, trained leaders, and specific functions that these leaders perform. Leadership is anything but simple, as many attend school for years to be able to lead these churches in the correct way and teach right doctrines. As a result, most believing participants are left to spectate, because leadership is so complex.

In a movement model, all believers are active participants in all levels of church life. While they are learning best practices, they are actually also leading others. The meetings are highly participatory, and the Bible discussions involve everyone. Because these meetings take place in the home and in an environment of community, the new believers are doing church together in a way that fits their reality and, in fact, is reinforced by their context. New disciples of Jesus are learning to lead in simple ways so that when they share their newfound faith with a few of their friends or family, they can reproduce the simple kind of church that they have been involved in leading.

This also applies to central sacraments of the Christian faith: baptism and observing the Lord's Supper. In Cuba, a few years ago, I interviewed the president of a prominent denomination. The church in Cuba had been experiencing an explosion of growth in the past decade, and churches were spilling into home-based groups because there weren't enough facilities to hold the believers. I inquired as to who had the authority to baptize and learned that it was only ordained pastors. The president told me that the denominational leadership wanted to release the "lay leaders" to baptize new converts, but the pastors had voted against the idea. They stated that if the lay people wanted to be qualified to baptize, then they should go through the hard work of completing a seminary degree, as the pastors had done.

I asked how many people were waiting to be baptized, and the breathtaking answer was eighty thousand! There were about 250 pastors across the island, and they simply could not keep up with what the Spirit of God was doing. I wondered what the number of believers would look like if those eighty thousand were baptizing their friends and relatives instead of being put into a holding pattern and taught that they weren't "qualified" to baptize others.

Our research has clearly found that releasing all believers to baptize releases movements. House-church participants who have no formal seminary training or denominational credentials are empowered to baptize those whom they lead to Jesus. Research shows that 60 percent of the churches that released everyone to baptize new converts saw more than twenty baptisms per year, but a much smaller percentage of the churches who required special training saw the same results. The goal here is simple: to point to the evidence. When people are released to baptize new converts without having to wait upon an ordained pastor, movements are freed to move.

When we train leaders who are developing the 5-5-5 networks of house churches, we emphasize the simplicity of baptism. The baptism passages in Acts reveal that the early church practiced immediate baptism. There was no delay between people recognizing Jesus as Lord and their being baptized.

We might consider that the most visible leader of the early church, the Apostle Paul, did not perform all the baptisms in a church. Paul's clearest statement on this is found in 1 Corinthians, where he wrote,

> I thank God that I did not baptize any of you except Crispus and Gaius, so no one can say that you were baptized in my name. (Yes, I also baptized the household of Stephanas; beyond that, I don't remember if I baptized anyone else.) For Christ did not send me to baptize, but to preach the gospel—not with wisdom and eloquence, lest the cross of Christ be emptied of its power.
> —1 Corinthians 1:14–17

Even though Paul was the most prominent leader, he was not the one baptizing the new converts. The fact is that we don't have a lot of evidence in the New Testament record that reveals who actually baptized.

The same can be said of the Lord's Supper. If hundreds, if not thousands, of new converts meeting in homes are waiting for a specially trained leader to officiate the Lord's Supper, it is not very likely that they will have the blessing of sharing in this sacrament on a regular basis. In our movement we practice the remembrance of the Lord's death in simple ways that can be repeated by others after they participate in it.

Root Principle #2: Immediate Obedience

The second principle highlights how people in fast-growing movements respond in faith. They don't wait until they attain a certain level of maturity before they begin to obey the commands of Christ. They obey immediately upon turning to him.

> On the surface, this might not seem significant, but from a statistical point of view, this is a strong predictor of what causes movement growth.

Over 55 percent of those who are strong in this factor see at least three churches started and over twenty people come to Christ in a year's time, while only 45 percent of those who are below average in the immediate response factor see similar results. On the surface, this might not seem significant, but from a statistical point of view, this is a strong predictor of what causes movement growth. And what's more, when you get into specific aspects of this factor, we see specific actions that are tied to movement growth. For instance, the following graph speaks to obedience as it relates to knowledge of the Bible. In churches where people memorize the Bible regularly, 98 percent of them see over twenty people come to Christ annually. Where this is lacking, so too are baptisms lacking.

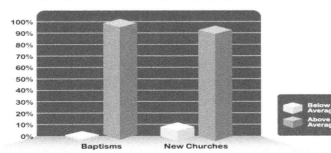

The faith of those within a movement is an active faith, not a passive, cognitive one. We train everyone who has been baptized to obey Christ by sharing their faith within their social network, as soon as possible, until five people respond to the gospel. As five people come to faith, they are immediately challenged to do the same with five more family members or friends, thus developing a multigenerational growth system based on swift conformity to the teachings of Jesus.

Immediate obedience depends on young disciples observing the obedience of those who have been following Christ for a longer period. It is a "do-as-I-do" life of faith, in which modeling and mentoring are built into the system. Obedience doesn't occur in isolation, but in community. People obey together, as they are learning from memorizing the Scriptures and following God's promptings together.

At the same time, we don't make obedience vague. Every new Christian is given a challenge of a practical way to obey. We encourage them to identity five people in their lives with whom they can share their story and the gospel of Jesus. This makes following Christ practical and gives them a way to act on the exciting transformation that they are experiencing as they discover relief from guilt and the joys of the Holy Spirit in their hearts. Being a disciple of Jesus and becoming a disciple-maker is a way of life.

Root Principle #3: Intentional Reproduction

When we analyzed the results from our research to find the factors that influenced baptisms and church starts, this factor rose to the top. While all seven factors work together to release a movement that moves, it's hard to ignore the fact that intentional reproduction stirs kingdom movements more than any other. Churches that emphasize this principle have more baptisms and produce more churches.

If churches responded to our questions related to this factor with either high or very high responses, then they were much more likely to see baptisms and new church starts. In our surveys we asked various questions about things that leaders did and did not do that focused their ministry on intentional reproduction. We asked about how new disciples are encouraged to start churches in their homes. This question reveals that there is a significant impact that this action has upon both baptisms and church plants, as you can see in the chart on the following page.

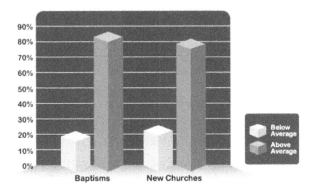

NEW DISCIPLES ARE ENCOURAGED TO START CHURCHES IN THEIR HOMES

About 80 percent of the churches that are high in this category saw at least twenty baptisms per year and started three new churches.

All are called to reproduce and make disciples. This is not the job of a few who are set apart. The entire church is involved. Practically, this means that everything we do is designed to be reproduced. If a leader of a large network of churches gathers his key leaders together, that time is constructed in such a way that they can repeat it with others. And then those others can repeat it. Everything is reproducible, even to the point that a new Christian can experience it and then repeat it.

Root Principle #4: Relational Discipleship

The church universal agrees that discipleship is important. However, the form that discipleship takes is another matter altogether. In a movement context, discipleship takes on a specific shape that both empowers the disciple to do the works of Christ and trains them in those works.

When the word *discipleship* is used, it most often connotes activities that are cognitive in nature. We might think of discipleship in terms of curriculum to study or books to read.

However, movement discipleship occurs through life-on-life interaction and depends on the newer follower of Christ sharing and modeling. This leads to transformative change that is motivating a loving response. The Spirit of God working through people is the primary resource.

As the next graph demonstrates, 72 percent of those who were high in this factor see over twenty baptisms per year, while only 28 percent of those who do not embrace this principle see anything close to these kinds of results.

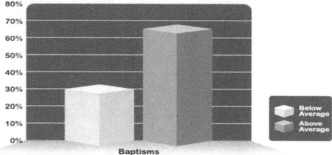

Then when we look at a specific aspect of this factor, we can see the impact of specific actions. We asked church leaders if they intentionally build relationships with those who have been recently baptized to show the way that we make new disciples. Over 70 percent of those who responded positively see at least three new churches started per year. And since everything, including starting new churches, is done through relational connections, the way that new Christians are discipled fits that form of starting new churches.

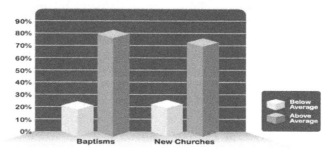

Modeling and mentoring are the way that discipleship happens, just as Paul wrote in 2 Timothy 2:2: "And the things you have heard me say in the presence of many witnesses entrust to reliable people who will also be qualified to teach others." Paul showed Timothy what to do and then Timothy passed that on to others.

This means that our discipleship does not occur in a classroom and is not dependent upon written resources. We have people at every level modeling how to live (and follow Christ) for others. Discipleship is illustrated and then explained so that it can be repeated. Then, when people do it themselves, feedback is given. This pushes discipleship out to the fringes, to the level of the new Christian, so that everyone gets involved.

Root Principle #5: Passionate Prayer

The church is not lacking in teaching about the importance of prayer. In movements, prayer is part of the atmosphere of their way of life, more than a topic to be studied. When churches pray with passion they see more baptisms and church plants, as the graph below demonstrates.

If we get concrete, we see the importance that specific aspects of prayer have on the life of movements. For instance, 74 percent of those who spend time daily in prayer with others see at least three churches started every year, while only about 26 percent of those who do not pray in this way see that kind of growth.

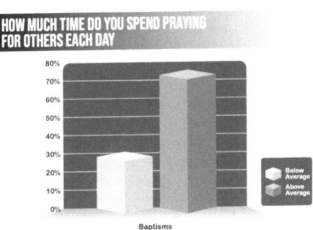

Prayer for the lost, for other leaders, for the redemption of entire groups of people, for leaders within a community, for those being persecuted—these are the things that drive movements. Even more, we see prayer for healing, for miracles, and for God's intervention answered regularly. A Jesus movement is far more than a strategy that we employ. Our strategies are our way of getting involved with God, as we seek his face. This section is short because much has been written on prayer. Just know that we see prayer as critical to the life of a successful movement.

Root Principle #6: Continual Empowerment

Movements that move must be fed or the movement will dissipate. Our research reveals that continual training feeds movements. Churches that responded with high scores in this factor had more baptisms and more church plants.

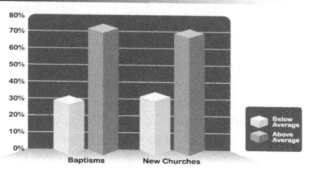

Too often the focus on equipping dissipates after a Christian reaches an acceptable level of maturity. As long as they attend church regularly and volunteer consistently, then they are left to themselves. That approach is not taken in movements.

The goal is to empower everyone to continue to grow and flourish in their walk with Christ. As Paul said in his letter to the Philippians:

> I want to know Christ—yes, to know the power of his resurrection and participation in his sufferings, becoming like him in his death, and so, somehow, attaining to the resurrection from the dead.
>
> Not that I have already obtained all this, or have already arrived at my goal, but I press on to take hold of that for which Christ Jesus took hold of me. Brothers and sisters, I do not consider myself yet to have taken hold of it. But one thing I do: Forgetting what is behind and straining toward what is ahead, I press on toward the goal to win the prize for which God has called me heavenward in Christ Jesus. —Philippians 3:10–14

Even at the end of his ministry, Paul was pressing on for more, and the goal within a movement is to set up a way that this mindset can be fostered through every stage of life for everyone. For instance, a regular practice is training to share Christ.

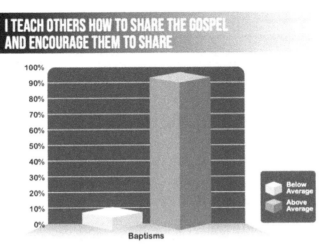

Notice that when making disciples and training them to share what has happened to them in their social networks, about 94 percent of them see at least twenty baptisms per year. When training is not done, they only see, on average, one baptism per year.

Continual empowerment is woven into the life of these churches. Movement leaders receive ongoing, just-in-time training that equips them in the midst of the challenges that they face. They never graduate to the point that they no longer receive practical, biblical equipping for the work of ministry. We do this through learning communities where all of our leaders receive ongoing, continual training. Leadership development, a challenge in all movements, happens in learning communities. This is so significant and so simple, but many miss this key element, and thus they miss the crucial principle of continually instilling their leaders with the flow of God's power.

Root Principle #7: Strategic Networking

While the first six principles are organic in nature, the seventh is strategic. It's not mechanical in that it is performed from a detached base of operation, like a missionary headquarters. It operates within the life of the simple churches themselves, but those involved seek the Spirit's leading regarding how to share the gospel along new lines of relationships. About 64 percent of those who do this well see at least three new churches started annually, as the graph on the following page shows.

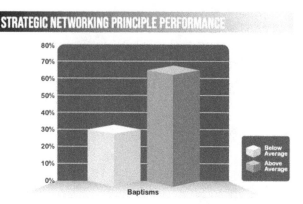

This is what the New Testament identifies as apostolic work, where house churches send out those who are called to venture into new areas and identify a "person of peace" who is open to the gospel and has influence within a community.

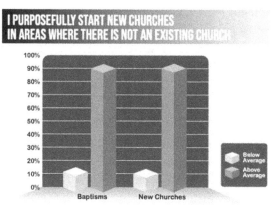

Ninety percent of the churches who seek to start new churches in areas where there is not an existing church saw at least twenty baptisms and three new churches in a given year. They don't wait for people to come to them. They extend out into new spaces and watch how the Spirit will move through them.

One key practice that releases this principle is finding a "person of peace." This is a person who is open to the gospel and has influence within a community. When such a person is reached, then a multigenerational 5-5-5 network can be started, resulting in 155 new believers and 20–25 new house churches. This leads to large numbers of new disciple-makers and then the repetition of the process: find a new person of peace and start a new 5-5-5 network. We do not try to extract individuals out of their communities in order to become Christians. We seek to reach them within their already established social networks. Sharing Jesus through the persons of peace fosters the spread of the gospel through relational networks in organic and natural ways that fit a local culture.

Conclusion

These are the seven root principles that have been statistically proven to promote kingdom movement life and growth. The roots establish a movement into the ground of Christ. From these roots arise the leadership practices that must be adopted so that what is developed in the roots is transferred to the fruit: growing it, nourishing it, and supporting it.

Chapter 7

Leadership Best Practice #1: Depend upon the Presence and Power of the Spirit

Introduction

Often a missionary or pastor will contact me to explore what it might look like for me to help them develop a movement of their own. These conversations frequently follow a similar pattern. Whether we meet in person or over a video conference, they inquire about strategies for getting started, and usually we discuss the seven root principles introduced in the previous chapter. As we talk, I find myself shifting the conversation away from a focus on methodology to telling my own story about how I got involved in movement work. I share that I didn't begin with inquiring about movement strategies, but with prayer—in fact, several years of prayer.

As I approached the watershed moment of my fiftieth birthday, I spent six months seeking the Lord for direction about the balance of my ministry and life. Earnestly asking him to show me what he wanted me to focus my work on, I waited on the Lord. During this season of life, I was reminded of previous visits to Yoido Full Gospel Church's Prayer Mountain in Seoul, Korea, where people were fasting and praying for up to forty days in little grottos on the hillsides. The intensity of the presence of God on that mountain was extraordinary. Dr. Cho and Dr. John Hurston had built the largest church in the world through focused prayer, inspiring me to fast and pray for guidance.

My mind and heart were flooded with memories of visits around the world with various leaders of God's people. There was a visit to Deeper Life Church in Lagos, Nigeria, which today has three million members around the world. At the time of my visit in the 1980s, they had a massive building that would hold tens of thousands. Prayer was a centerpiece of Dr. Kumuyi's life and ministry. I remembered the experience of leading Dr. John Maxwell and his church staff through that enormous church auditorium as we discussed the impact that Dr. Kumuyi, the math professor turned pastor, was having on Nigeria through prayer.

As these memories came to me, I decided to spend six months prayerfully seeking God's will for my future. As I prayed, a petition came into focus: "Lord, help me have the greatest impact possible on where the largest number of people possible spend eternity." After finding God's guidance, I prayed this prayer passionately for many years, with the understanding that using the word *possible* opened the door of faith to what God could do—rather than just what my limited gifts and talents could achieve. *Possible* is a significant word of open-ended potential, intentionally used twice to ask God to do something far beyond what we mortals could "ask, think, or imagine" (Eph 3:20).

I have not developed a large ministry base in the United States. I don't even have a staff. Instead, we are a group of part-time helpers and a large international network of friends and fellow travelers seeking to serve God. What can one man—an introvert who doesn't have the gift of evangelism—do to impact the world for Christ? The years of intensive prayers were answered gradually, with the Holy Spirit giving me specific step-by-step guidance that led me into movement work. At the beginning of this prayer journey, only in my greatest hopes and dreams did I imagine seeing over one million souls brought into eternal life with Jesus Christ. Fifteen years later that hope became a reality, and now we are dreaming of five to ten million new believers.

> God's guidance led me to connect with the right people—who lent their expertise to develop an understanding of what drives a movement—at the right time.

The Holy Spirit is very practical. His leading of individuals in the Scriptures are replete with instruction and guidance, including Moses at the burning bush, Joshua at Jericho, Gideon with his men at the stream drinking water, and Esther, as she intervened to save the Jewish nation. Although I would never think of myself as a great leader, still he patiently answered my faith yearnings and specifically led me into doing statistical research on movements, partnering with experts in this field to determine how our beliefs and practices impact growth results. God's guidance led me to connect with the right people—who lent their expertise to develop an understanding of what drives a movement—at the right time. This journey was extraordinary and supernatural, and the results speak for themselves. If the Lord did that for me, he will also guide you as you diligently seek his face.

There are many moving parts to walking with the Spirit. Learning to hear and recognize God's voice is critical. Obedience to what he says to do is foundational. It's like football practice in the summer months when "two-a-day practices" focus on the fundamentals. I can still hear my football coach teaching us how to block and tackle, repeatedly at every practice. Hearing the voice of God in our hearts is one of those fundamentals we need to practice every day.

> His will is that we exercise faith, and by faith working through love he can do extraordinary things with ordinary people.

When we read Jesus's words, "My sheep listen to my voice; I know them, and they follow me" (John 10:27), most of us really don't know how to hear him, and we struggle to find his guidance when making important life decisions. Friends often tell me that I have a strong intuitive sense of what to do. This is not intuition; it's hearing and obeying God's voice. And it can become our lifestyle and lead us into his amazing will for our lives. His will is that we exercise faith, and by faith working through love he can do extraordinary things with ordinary people.

About thirty years ago, I met with a spiritually mature woman, who led an orphanage in Haiti, who told me a story that illustrates this point. She had a need for $41,500 for the children and was meeting in Oklahoma with the leader of an internationally known television ministry. He invited her to share the financial needs of her orphanage with him. She told him this: "If the Lord has laid it on your heart to help us, he will tell you how much we need." As she related the story, this well-known Christian minister turned his office chair toward the wall and prayed quietly for a few minutes. Then, without speaking, he wrote her a check for $41,500. This brother had mastered the fundamentals of hearing and obeying the Spirit.

Hearing most obviously includes reading and obeying the written Word of God, but we also need to learn to listen to the Spirit's voice in our hearts and minds as we seek his guidance. When the pillar of cloud by day and the pillar of fire by night led the former slaves, the Israelites, through the desert, the guidance was clear and specific. However, under the New Covenant, we have to find God's leading without a physical pillar of cloud by day and pillar of fire by night. This is a process. It takes time and focus on our part. We must be willing to make personal sacrifices and to put his voice and guidance above our own.

Learning to walk in intimacy with the Spirit is not easy or cheap. Jesus nailed it when he said that we must die to ourselves to truly live. Finding his voice among the many competing voices of self and culture is definitely challenging for each of us. When we pay the price to learn the fundamentals, we are laying a foundation for the central practice of movement work.

The Centrality of the Work of the Spirit

Victor John helped initiate one of the largest and earliest movements in India. He shared with me how over eleven million people had been baptized through his movement networks since he first began this work in the late 1990s. He expressed a sense of awe and wonder about how God has moved far beyond what could be controlled, counted, or organized. He said to me, "This is a work of God, but I often find that people come to me and want to copy my strategy without any real commitment to walking in the life of the Spirit."

 Of the seven leadership "best practices" that this book introduces, "Depend upon the Presence and Power of the Spirit" is the most central.

We are experiencing today what the resurrected Jesus promised to his disciples, "You will receive power when the Holy Spirit comes on you; and you will be my witnesses in Jerusalem, and in all Judea and Samaria, and to the ends of the earth" (Acts 1:8). I am a witness to the fact that God has been at work in our movements in Southeast Asia and West Africa. Without the outpouring of the Spirit, we would not have experienced the huge numbers of transformed lives that we have seen. I am humbled to play a part.

Of the seven leadership "best practices" that this book introduces, "Depend upon the Presence and Power of the Spirit" is the most central. Such encouragements and exhortations are commonplace. Many resources, especially Curtis Sergeant's book, *The Only One: Living Fully In, By, and For God*,[1] give practical and detailed instruction on how to walk with the Spirit of God daily.

As you read this book, you might be tempted to offer a quick "Amen" and then move on to organizational issues. But to do so misses the point. This best practice is not just central because the Bible claims it to be so. It is central because it lies at the center of the other six best practices. Or to put it another way, the work of the Spirit shapes how the other six best practices operate. We might imagine it using the following diagram.

---

1 Sergeant, *The Only One*.

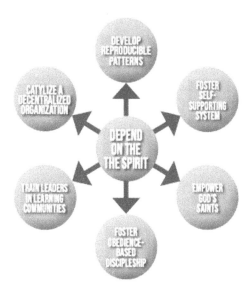

The work of the Spirit is the "operating system" running in the background of our lives and of a movement. Like a good computer OS, it may be silent and not easily observed, but it impacts every action and result. Without the Spirit as our OS, we are humans trying to do God's work with human energy and effort. It may have the appearance of religion, but without the power and presence of the Holy Spirit, when it comes to the transference of the gospel into another culture and the long-term sustainability of disciple-making and leadership development, human effort alone will fail.

In this paradigm of the best practices which I have observed in our work, as the Spirit feeds and energizes the other six best practices, we see that the other six point back to and promote the work of the Spirit. Transference and sustainability of best practices is our great challenge. Without focus and the daily training of disciple-makers in this first best practice, we will shorten the reach and the life of our movements. This is not simply a topic that we acknowledge theologically and then move on to practical leadership issues. It has practical implications through and through.

Where to Begin?

Now when it comes to the Holy Spirit, I recognize that there are many different perspectives. I am not here to argue the merits of the various theological points of view. There are plenty of excellent resources that explore these matters. I will mention that I have found any of Derek Prince's resources to be invaluable. In what follows, I'm simply providing observations that serve as testimony regarding what is transpiring in our movements. I am pointing to how God is at work and how movement leaders are getting involved with that work.

> "My Father is always at work to this very day, and I too am working" (John 5:17).
> If God is always at work, then movement work does not begin with our efforts, our organization, or our strategies.

In fact, this is exactly how Jesus described his own ministry in John 5:16 and following. In response to Jesus's healing on the Sabbath, the religious leaders of the day challenged his theology about how and when God works. He stated, "My Father is always at work to this very day, and I too am working" (John 5:17). These words only resulted in further theological dispute, as the Jewish leaders wanted to kill him because he was "making himself equal with God." They wanted to debate how God can do the things that God might want to do, when in fact, they were missing the fact that God was doing them right before their eyes.

Depending upon the Spirit involves seeing what God is doing in the world. If God is always at work, then movement work does not begin with our efforts, our organization, or our strategies. It begins with asking the Spirit to give us eyes to see the good works of our Father. To do otherwise is to get the starting point wrong and miss what the Father is about. We might have good intentions because we want to see people come to a saving knowledge of Christ, but our efforts for seeing this come to fruition will fall short if we fail to begin with this basic principle of the Spirit: look and see. Henry Blackaby summarizes this approach by saying, "Watch to see where God is working and join Him in His work."

Moving into dependence upon the Spirit can lead us to join in on what God is doing. In response to the debate with his religious contemporaries, Jesus said, "Very truly I tell you, the Son can do nothing by himself; he can do only what he sees his Father doing, because whatever the Father does the Son also does" (John 5:19). Jesus saw and then joined in with the Father. This is a remarkable claim. Jesus did not act on his own. He gave his life for others while walking with the Father through the Holy Spirit's leading. If this was the case for the second person of the Holy Trinity, why should it not be the case for us today?

I sometimes share how young Christians who are oral learners can become leaders of gatherings comprised of people whom they have led to Christ, occasionally within days after their own conversion. "How does this happen? What training have you developed? How do you avoid false teaching?" I could be asked. "This is happening right before my eyes. Praise

God!" It is happening because these young converts, who may be in their sixties, are seeing and experiencing Christ's power and the presence of the Spirit in their life in real time. This isn't a confirmation class that imparts knowledge; rather this is a new convert reading the Sermon on the Mount and obeying what they read. For example, Jesus's command to "Love your enemies" becomes a serious challenge when you are being persecuted. Relying on the Spirit, these believers press into God's power to overcome the fear, hatred, and other temptations to go back to their old life. In this reality, instruction from the Bible is practical; and with the Spirit's help, it brings life transformation, not just Bible knowledge.

What the Spirit Is Doing in China and within Islam

I pray that God will open our eyes to see what he is doing around the world. Honestly, it's mind-boggling. In chapter 1 we briefly introduced how Christianity spread throughout China while Chinese political leaders were working to shut it down. A very brief historical look could start at Mao's takeover of China, after Western missionaries were sent home and Chairman Mao's wife announced that to learn about Christianity in China in the future you would need to visit a museum.

Meanwhile, movements of viral faith were bubbling up. Fenggang Yang, of Purdue University's Center on Religion and Chinese Society, estimates that there are between 93 million and 115 million Protestants in China, with fewer than 30 million attending officially registered churches. Yang projects that only "modest" continued growth would result in 160 million Christians by 2025 and 247 million by 2030.[2]

A high percentage of these Christians are presently part of movements, having been birthed out of underground, illegal movements that were developed during the twentieth century.[3]

When I first met Ying Kai, author of *T4T: A Discipleship ReRevolution*, in 2000 in Hong Kong and heard how he was seeing so many come to Christ in China, I saw a man who was not focused on promoting a church strategy so that the Chinese church could thrive. He spoke of seeing thousands responding to the gospel every month. Later, I learned that this man of prayer was deeply connected to the Lord and walked very passionately and closely with the Spirit. He infused that lifestyle in his leaders, and it was passed from generation to generation.

Lord, open our eyes.

---

2 Albert, "Christianity in China."
3 Albert.

Equally surprising as the work of the Spirit in China is the current stirring within traditionally Muslim communities. As David Garrison has observed in his book, *A Wind in the House of Islam: How God Is Drawing Muslims around the World to Faith in Jesus Christ*, a major shift is currently transpiring. Whereas few Muslims have responded with faith to the gospel historically, now many movements have arisen. Garrison writes,

> In Islam's first 12 centuries we found no voluntary, and only a handful of coerced, conversions to the Christian religion. Not until the end of the 19th century, twelve and a half centuries after the death of Muhammad, did we find the first voluntary movements of Muslims to Christ that number at least 1,000 baptisms.[4]

The Spirit is moving in a different way today. Garrison continues:

> In only the first 12 years of the 21st century, an additional 69 movements to Christ of at least 1,000 baptized Muslim-background believers or 100 new worshipping fellowships have appeared. These 21st-century movements are not isolated to one or two corners of the world. They are taking place throughout the House of Islam: in sub-Saharan Africa, in the Persian world, in the Arab world, in Turkestan, in South Asia and in Southeast Asia. Something is happening—something historic, something unprecedented.[5]

Lord, open our eyes.

Jerry Trousdale observes that his organization's work in West Africa has resulted in what he calls "unprecedented" impact upon Muslim communities. These include things like:

- multiple cases of entire mosques coming to faith in Christ;
- thousands of ordinary men and women being used by God to achieve seemingly impossible outcomes;
- tens of thousands of Muslim-background Christians becoming dedicated intercessors who fast and pray for the gospel to penetrate their community;
- Muslim people groups that never had even one church among them now have more than fifty churches planted, and in some cases more than one hundred churches—within two years of engagement; and
- former sheikhs, imams, and militant Islamists making up 20 percent or more of the new Christian leaders in Muslim regions.[6]

---

4 Garrison, *Wind in the House of Islam*, 18.
5 Garrison, 18.
6 Trousdale, *Miraculous Movements*, 24–25.

Garrison and Trousdale wrote these observations in 2014, and I am a witness to this continuing work among Muslim people through our movements. It is not uncommon for an Imam to come to faith in Christ and for many of his followers to quickly believe and be baptized soon thereafter. In this era the Spirit is making unique inroads into people groups who are hungry for God's truth and grace.

I personally know a Suffi Imam who had over two thousand Muslim disciples and who then came to faith in Christ and led many of his followers to Jesus. He now has a dynamic healing ministry and is well known in his region. People come to his home and wait for hours for him to pray for their healing. At one gathering of disciple-makers, a friend asked this brother how he was saved, and the former Imam looked him in the eye and said, "By the blood of Jesus and *only* by the blood of Jesus!"

Lord, open our eyes.

Another Sufi Imam left his large following and began to preach the gospel publicly, instead of working through the 5-5-5 system of disciple-making. He was beaten so many times that he finally gave up public speaking and carries in his body the wounds and permanent injuries of his testimony for Christ.

> It is a countercultural journey. One of the key leaders in our movement had his beard plucked out after he was baptized.

It is common for those who believe to experience persecution because of their faith. It is a countercultural journey. One of the key leaders in our movement had his beard plucked out after he was baptized. Some have had the water cut off to their fields and yet have reaped a larger harvest than their unbelieving neighbors. One old couple had their house set on fire while they were sleeping; fortunately, a neighbor boy woke them up and saved their lives. Another brother was tied to a pole and publicly beaten.

The Spirit is at work, yet there is a cost for those who are joining the kingdom of God. These people, many of whom are my personal friends, are living the words of Paul: "Everyone who wants to live a godly life in Christ Jesus will be persecuted" (2 Tim 3:12).

A Look Inside

Seeing what God is doing in China and in the world of Islam offers us a high-level picture of the work of the Holy Spirit in movements. But when we move from the thirty-thousand-feet level to the grassroots, we see that much is going on. Jesus's claims about how he does what he sees the Father doing were rooted in a specific, local action with a man who needed a touch from God. In the same way, the Spirit is working in the context of cities, towns, and villages from person to person, revealing the love of Christ, often with the testimony of believers being accompanied by signs and wonders.

Raipur lives in a rural area of India called Aamir. He met a man named Samar, who was talking to his neighbor; and after a few conversations, he learned that Samar was a Christian. Over a period of weeks, Samar met with Raipur to tell him about Jesus; and eventually he became a follower of Christ. However, his wife and family refused to believe with him.

Raipur was an epileptic who had taken every treatment available to him, but nothing was working. He shared about his sickness with Samar, who told him to wait for a week until others could come and pray for him. When they arrived, these men prayed for Raipur for a few hours, while his family watched. While they were praying, he felt a change in his body; and he walked away healed from epilepsy, later confirmed by the doctors. After witnessing this specific work of God, Raipur was baptized and his wife and children believed and were baptized.

Kadir is a poor Muslim fisherman who was addicted to drugs and gambling. Very little of the money that he made from his business made it home to take care of his family. Osman told him about the gospel of Jesus Christ, to which he responded with curses and disrespect. However, Osman continued to pray for him and tell him about Jesus. After a few weeks, Kadir found himself in dire need of money to pay his mortgage and take his son to the doctor.

> This daily, grassroots dependence upon the power of the Spirit drives movement life, as real people are encountering God's power and love and are being transformed by the life and power of Jesus Christ.

Osman prayed for him and then shared the story of when Jesus said, "Come, follow me, and I will send you out to fish for people" (Matt 4:19). By the inspiration of the Holy Spirit, Osman told Kadir to go and cast his net. He then caught two times more fish than he had ever caught before. He then had enough money to pay the bank and take his son to the doctor, which he did not have to do because he soon learned that his son had been healed. This led to further conversations with Osman, and then Kadir and his family received Christ and were baptized.

Such stories of the acts of the Spirit lie at the heart of movement work, and they could be repeated endlessly. These are seemingly spectacular accounts involving common people who are seeing and joining what God is doing. This daily, grassroots dependence upon the power of the Spirit drives movement life, as real people are encountering God's power and love and are being transformed.

Waking Up

Honestly, what God is doing today he has done many times before. The book of Acts is an account of the acts of the Holy Spirit, full of dreams, visions, miracles, and healings—all for the sake of people coming to know of God's love. In addition, these acts have occurred in revival movements throughout church history. One of the most significant accounts is found in the ministry of John Wesley. In 1742, Wesley and a coworker named Mr. Meyrick caught a cold, from which Wesley recovered, but Meyrick did not. Wesley writes,

> When I came home, they told me the physician said he did not expect Mr. Meyrick would live till the morning. I went to him, but his pulse was gone. He had been speechless and senseless for some time. A few of us immediately joined in prayer: (I relate the naked fact:) Before we had done, his sense and his speech returned. Now he that will account for this by natural causes, has my free leave; but I choose to say, this is the power of God.

After his initial recovery, Mr. Meyrick faced a setback. Five days later, on Christmas day, Wesley reports:

> The physician told me he could do no more; Mr. Meyrick could not live over the night. I went up and found them all crying about him; his legs being cold, and (as it seemed) dead already. We all kneeled down and called upon God with strong cries and tears. He opened his eyes and called for me; and, from that hour he continued to recover his strength, till he was restored to perfect health. I wait to hear who will either disprove this fact or philosophically account for it.[7]

God is alive and at work in ways that don't always fit our expectations. One of the common ways that God has been moving is through dreams and visions, especially among Muslims. Trousdale writes,

> Of the former Muslim leaders who are now making disciples and planting churches, about 40 percent reported a dream or vision of Jesus that prompted them to begin to search to know more about Isa al Mesih (Jesus the Messiah). And the remarkable thing is that all of those dreams were unique to them. Even if many of the dreams include similar themes, the context and message are always different and relevant to each person having the dream. We have not recorded exactly the same dream twice.[8]

Joining God

The work of leading a movement is the work of facilitating space for the Holy Spirit. This is why this best practice lies at the center of all the others.

---

7 Cooke, "John Wesley Saw Some Crazy Miracles!"
8 John with Coles, *Bhojpuri Breakthrough*, 175.

The importance of prayer to the movement work cannot be overstated. Jesus spoke clearly to this in John 15:1–8.

> I am the true vine, and my Father is the gardener. He cuts off every branch in me that bears no fruit, while every branch that does bear fruit he prunes so that it will be even more fruitful. You are already clean because of the word I have spoken to you. Remain in me, as I also remain in you. No branch can bear fruit by itself; it must remain in the vine. Neither can you bear fruit unless you remain in me.
>
> I am the vine; you are the branches. If you remain in me and I in you, you will bear much fruit; apart from me you can do nothing. If you do not remain in me, you are like a branch that is thrown away and withers; such branches are picked up, thrown into the fire and burned. If you remain in me and my words remain in you, ask whatever you wish, and it will be done for you. This is to my Father's glory, that you bear much fruit, showing yourselves to be my disciples.

God wants us to bear much fruit, the fruit of the kingdom, but this is impossible unless we remain, or abide, in Jesus. Without this, we can "do nothing." Unless we learn to walk with God, we cannot do the things that God wants to do through us. This abiding occurs on four levels.

Level #1: Preparation

For ten years I felt led to pray repeatedly every day that God would open a door so that I could have the greatest impact possible upon where the largest number of people possible spend eternity. I was not motivated to pray this prayer by the need to start a movement. At that time, movements as we understand them today were not a known phenomenon. I was simply praying this because I felt compelled to do so.

> When pastors or missionaries want me to mentor them, one of the first things I want to know is how God has prepared them for this kind of work through times of prayer and their personal journey with Christ.

In retrospect, I now realize that God was shaping my heart through that prayer so that I would have the kind of focus that would align with movement work. It gave me a heart for people so that I could have the flexibility to listen, learn, and obey the Spirit as he led me step by step into the unknown, which became known as movement work. It shaped me to focus on God and his work, as opposed to focusing on what I could accomplish or making a name for myself. It sensitized me to the Spirit's specific guidance, as he led me into researching movements and then piloting a few.

When pastors or missionaries want me to mentor them, one of the first things I want to know is how God has prepared them for this kind of work through times of prayer and their personal journey with Christ. If this foundation is not laid, it will be too tempting to focus on human effort and our own self-aggrandizement, instead of looking to see what God is doing and giving him all the glory.

Level #2: Atmosphere of Prayer

Bill Smith is one of the most experienced leaders in movement work that I know. Few have had as much firsthand exposure to on-the-ground movement life or as much interaction with various movement leaders. In one of his trips to visit movements in China, he shared a hotel room for some time with Ying Kai. Bill tells of how Ying arose every morning at four o'clock to worship and pray for at least two hours. Bill listened to Ying pray for each of his key leaders by name, interceding specifically for their needs and for the Spirit's power to move through them.

In his subsequent interaction with movement leaders who were part of Ying Kai's networks, Bill saw the same kind of commitment to pray, both in duration and in specificity. As he interviewed them, Bill realized that most of them had never met Ying Kai and many did not even know his name. They were not praying this way because they had been taught to do so in a Bible school or church seminar. They did so because it had been modeled for them as Ying's lifestyle was passed down from one generation of leaders to the next. This is how movements move.

Prayer is part of the atmosphere of how people operate as the church. Everyone is involved in it. The words of Victor John reiterate this point:

> Prayer is the heartbeat of the movement. The believers pray passionately; it's part of their DNA. When the believers gather, everyone is allowed to pray. They don't just listen to a leader or the more mature believers pray. Sometimes it's special prayer and fasting with other believers; sometimes it's continual talking with God during all kinds of everyday activities. Prayer is not complicated and anybody can do it.[9]

Level #3: Intercession

In movements, there is a focus on intercession rooted in a belief that God is acting and will act in response to prayer. A Muslim convert name Rup had a neighbor named Sanjiban who had an accident that resulted in him being paralyzed. After learning of this, Rup and his family prayed for Sanjiban

---

9 John with Coles, *Bhojpuri Breakthrough*, 175.

during their family prayers, but God had more in mind. While trying to sleep, Rup sensed that the Spirit wanted to bring healing through him to Sanjiban. Therefore, he prepared himself in prayer and then went to Sanjiban's house to pray for him.

Rup massaged Sanjiban's head and hands with oil while he prayed, and he felt something happening. Rup asked Sanjiban to move his hands and open his mouth, which he could then do. Rup then massaged Sanjiban's body with oil and asked Sanjiban to pray with him in his mind, since he could not speak. For three hours Rup prayed. Then he asked Sanjiban to stand and walk, which to his surprise he was able to do. Sanjiban and his family were soon baptized.

Dr. J. Edwin Orr, a professor who taught about revivals at Wheaton College, took some of his students to England in 1940. While there, they visited the Epworth rectory that served as a home base for John Wesley. In the floor of Wesley's bedroom, near the bed, were two knee impressions that were made from his many hours of prayer.

When it was time to leave, one student was missing. Dr. Orr found the missing student with his knees filling those impressions, face down on the bed, praying, "Oh Lord, do it again! Do it again!" That student was Billy Graham!

Level #4: Prayer and Fasting

In addition to prayer and intercession, we need to adopt the discipline of fasting. Bill Bright wrote,

> According to Scripture, personal experience and observation, fasting and prayer can also effect change on a much grander scale. I am convinced that when God's people fast with a proper biblical motive—seeking God's face, not His hand—with a broken, repentant and contrite spirit, God will hear from heaven. He will heal our lives, our churches, our communities, our nation and our world. Fasting and prayer can bring about a change in the direction of our nation, the nations of the earth and the fulfillment of the Great Commission.[10]

I concur. When I travel among movement leaders, I generally spend seven days fasting before I depart. When we are facing special challenges in our movement, we encourage people to fast three times during the month. This discipline opens our eyes to see what the Spirit is doing, sharpens our ears to hear his voice, and charges our will to venture out into more radical obedience.

---

10 Bright, "Your Personal Guide to Fasting and Prayer."

Conclusion

This movement best practice of depending upon the power of the Spirit is not an item to put on your daily to-do list. It requires a lifestyle shift so that prayer becomes a doorway for remaining in Christ, which results in the experience of the Spirit being your "teacher," as Jesus taught in John 16.

Chapter 8

Leadership Best Practice #2: Catalyze a Decentralized Movement

Introduction

The history of the church is often viewed as a series of events carried by heroic figures. Biographies of larger than life church leaders inspire us, as they preach the gospel in new ways, carry the truth into new fields, and establish new traditions. Where would the church be today if Augustine had not written his *Confessions*, if Martin Luther had not nailed his "Ninety-Five Theses" to the Wittenberg door, if William Carey had remained a shoemaker instead of going to India and becoming the "father of modern Protestant missions," or if David Yonggi Cho had resigned his pastoral role after experiencing burnout instead of building the world's largest church through cell groups.

Even today, various streams of the church are seen as movements led by uniquely talented and charismatic individuals. They are set apart because of their oratory skills, the ability to cast clear vision, and commonly their attractiveness on camera, along with their passion for the gospel. They most often sit at the pinnacle of a top-down, centralized, command-and-control organization. God uses such leaders in amazing ways, but Jesus movements operate differently.

While capable leaders carry and communicate vision for the most significant movements around the world, as I have dug into how movements have arisen, developed, and been sustained over the last thirty years, I have not been able to identify any singular figure who could be highlighted as the figurehead leader of modern Jesus movements. There is no heroic figure like Martin Luther. In addition, in movements that possess the most sustaining power, there is no singular figure who orchestrates everything from the top.

There are leaders and usually a key leader of leaders, but they lead through a decentralized system that does not highlight the work of the people at the top of a leadership pyramid. Instead of a command-and-control system, they have developed a decentralized way of operating that facilitates the movement of the Spirit throughout the entire network of churches. We have learned how to organize our system so that we don't have to depend upon one person or even one set of leaders who are uniquely designed to lead a large organization.

We call what we do the 5-5-5 system, which I will describe at the end of this chapter. Let me encourage you, however, to work through these introductory sections, because our specific method for fostering a decentralized organization only works because we have fostered a decentralized culture that aligns with that strategy. Culture determines everything. Someone once said that culture eats strategy for breakfast! I think that another way of looking at Christ's mission of bringing the kingdom of God (the reign of God) to the earth is to think in terms of Christ bringing heaven's culture to the earth.

Jesus and Decentralized Culture

When Jesus walked the earth, the Jews of his day were waiting for a Messiah. In their view of what this meant, they were expecting a Messiah who would reign in the same way that King David led Israel, thereby returning them to their days of glory. N. T. Wright explains that this meant three things. First, Jerusalem would be restored to its glory as the center of God's blessing and activity. Second, the Romans would be driven out by the might of the Messiah's leadership. Third, the presence of God would return to the temple in Jerusalem.[1] The people of Israel in Jesus's time expected God to work in a centralized way, with one person and one place serving as the center around which all else would revolve.

Of course, this does not at all correlate with the way Jesus operated as the Messiah. Instead of being established on a throne, he was crucified on a hill outside of Jerusalem's city gates. Instead of raising up an army to conquer the Romans and drive them out of Israel, he taught his followers to love their enemies. Instead of rebuilding the temple to establish its grandeur and escorting the presence of God into a centralized place of worship, he taught that the time had come for true worship to be in Spirit and in truth, not in a certain location. Jesus's way of doing things did not meet man's way of doing things.

Even though people tried to elevate the status of Jesus to that of a ruler over people, and even though the disciples kept pushing him to meet common expectations, he constantly fought against what they wanted him to be. James and John asked Jesus if they could sit on the right and the left of him when he came into his glory, which meant that they were asking if they could be key power brokers in his kingdom (see Mark 10:35–45). He was standing against

---

1 Wright, *Jesus and the Victory of God*, 206.

the culture of the way things were supposed to be during that time, which are the same issues we humans deal with today.

In John 13 we see Jesus illustrating this stand against human culture and human nature.

> Jesus knew that the Father had put all things under his power, and that he had come from God and was returning to God; so he got up from the meal, took off his outer clothing, and wrapped a towel around his waist. After that, he poured water into a basin and began to wash his disciples' feet, drying them with the towel that was wrapped around him. ...
>
> When he had finished washing their feet, he put on his clothes and returned to his place. "Do you understand what I have done for you?" he asked them. "You call me 'Teacher' and 'Lord,' and rightly so, for that is what I am. Now that I, your Lord and Teacher, have washed your feet, you also should wash one another's feet. I have set you an example that you should do as I have done for you. Very truly I tell you, no servant is greater than his master, nor is a messenger greater than the one who sent him. Now that you know these things, you will be blessed if you do them."
> —John 13:3–5, 12–17

The action of Jesus washing his disciples' feet begins after his statement about the power and authority of the Father being given to him. Jesus didn't wash his disciples' feet out of powerlessness. He expressed his power through serving, just as Paul poetically stated that Jesus "made himself nothing by taking the very nature of a servant" (Phil 2:7).

> Jesus didn't wash his disciples' feet out of powerlessness. He expressed his power through serving.

While the way of man is to use power for command and control, Jesus used his power to serve, to put himself in the position of the lowest standing in the community. He was establishing an unexpected way of being the Messiah, and thereby an unexpected manifestation of the kingdom of God. Jesus not only took the lowest position; he demonstrated his love for the "least of these" by hanging out with sinners—the Samaritan woman and others who were rejected by the religious class. He brought the culture of the kingdom of heaven to the least.

Sadly, it seems that far too often leaders of God's people fail to embrace the spirit of the kingdom culture that Jesus initiated. He didn't tell his disciples to observe how he washed their feet and then go out and promote his name while making themselves great in the eyes of men and women. He said, "If I do this, you should do likewise."

This is the way of kingdom leadership. It's the way of kingdom movements. And we "will be blessed" if we embrace this way of life, even if it doesn't make sense. Jesus came to bring the culture of heaven to the earth. "No one can see the kingdom of God unless they are born again," Jesus told Nicodemus (John 3:3). If we are not born from heaven, servitude of all seems to be backwards thinking. Isn't the goal to be successful and have people serve us? Not in the kingdom of heaven.

In our experience of being God's leaders in a kingdom movement, we have been led to reflect on the prophetic works recorded in Isaiah about how God works:

> "For my thoughts are not your thoughts,
> neither are your ways my ways,"
> declares the LORD.
> "As the heavens are higher than the earth,
> so are my ways higher than your ways
> and my thoughts than your thoughts." (Isaiah 55:8–9)

The way of washing feet runs in the opposite direction of the typical way of leading where the few—and sometimes the one—operate within a command-and-control structure. But if you fail to see and embrace this foot-washing kingdom culture, the lure of power will serve as a magnet that will undermine movement life. Let me be clear: A command-and-control leadership culture will disempower Jesus movements.

Turn the Ship Around

The principle of leading by developing a decentralized system is illustrated by the experience of Navy Captain David Marquet in his book, *Turn the Ship Around*.[2] He was given charge of the worst-performing nuclear submarine in his fleet, the USS Santa Fe. His commander challenged him to see if he could pull this group out of the muck and mire of wallowing at the bottom of every performance metric and make it a sub that could do what it was designed to do.

When he arrived and began to assess the situation, Captain Marquet found a group of officers and sailors who had been berated and belittled to the point that they had no vision beyond trying to survive. In fact, when he would walk around and ask people what they did in their jobs, the common response was something like, "Whatever they tell me to do." It was the ultimate example of a command-and-control culture where the officers at the top controlled every detail.

---

2 Marquet, *Turn the Ship Around*.

Captain Marquet confronted Navy, top-down culture and listened to his officers and sailors, trying to understand what they wanted to see and do within their domains of responsibility. He then challenged them to become proactive, instead of reactive, so that they might become initiators of action on the ship instead of just doing what they were told. While he didn't deconstruct the official chain-of-command structure of a submarine, he did lead in a way that gave his crew more authority over their domain and dared them to lead themselves. He had the heart of a servant-commander, empowering his people instead of dominating them.

> To lead in the way of Jesus we must first confront our own human nature, our own desire for power and position.

This idea of a decentralized organization directly correlates with the best practice that I call "Empower," which we will discuss in chapter 11. In that chapter I will be laying out more from the experiences and insights of Captain Marquet and how they apply to the life of a kingdom movement. To lead in the way of Jesus we must first confront our own human nature, our own desire for power and position.

The Starfish and the Kingdom of God

In 2006, Ori Brafman and Rod Beckstrom published a business book about decentralized organizations. They wrote, "A centralized organization is easy to understand. … Whether you're a Spanish general, an Aztec leader, or a CEO of a Fortune 500 company, you use command-and-control to keep order in your organization, to make it efficient, and to function from day to day."[3] Brafman and Beckstrom found in their research of modern businesses, as well as in their study of historical experiences, that decentralized groups operate differently.

They tell the story of how the Spanish invaded the Americas in the sixteenth century and quickly defeated the Aztecs and the Incas by simply killing their leaders. These were both developed civilizations who had massive empires and great wealth, but they crumbled because their heads got cut off. In contrast, the Spanish couldn't defeat the Apaches in Northern Mexico and what is today New Mexico, even though they didn't have massive rooms full of gold and cities with great pyramids. The Apaches didn't have a head—a central leader who controlled everything—to cut off. Their decentralized way of operating catalyzed an environment where the Spanish were not able to defeat them for over two hundred years.

---

3 Brafman and Beckstrom, *Starfish and Spider*, 19.

Brafman and Beckstrom observed,

> In a decentralized organization, there's no clear leader, no hierarchy, and
> no headquarters. If and when a leader does emerge, that person has little
> power over others. The best that person can do to influence people is lead
> by example. … This doesn't mean that a decentralized system is the same
> as anarchy. There are rules and norms, but these aren't enforced by any one
> person. Rather, the power is distributed among all the people and across
> geographic regions.[4]

They entitled their book *The Starfish and the Spider* because a spider
can easily be killed by simply cutting off its head. However, a starfish cannot
be killed by cutting off any of its parts. In fact, if you cut a starfish in half,
its DNA will reproduce itself to the point of generating two starfish. "The
starfish doesn't have a head. Its central body isn't even in charge. In fact, the
major organs are replicated throughout each and every arm."[5]

Brafman and Beckstrom cite Alcoholics Anonymous as an example of
a decentralized organization. When its founder, Bill Wilson, saw that his
process for overcoming addiction could be multiplied and that people from
all over the world wanted to replicate it, he had a choice. He could create
a pyramid, with him at the top, and control how everyone operated, or he
could facilitate circles, a more democratic approach, allowing people to take
his principles and apply them in a variety of ways. He opted for the later.

"At Alcoholics Anonymous, no one's in charge. And yet, at the same time,
everyone's in charge."[6] The only thing that is consistent is the 12-step process,
but how groups implement it depends upon those who are involved. Bill
Wilson trusted each chapter, which operates in circles, to do what fits their
situation, instead of trying to set tight management systems that determine
exactly who and how the circles operate.

The experience of AA has many parallels with the decentralized
organization in our movement. We provide basic principles for how people
meet and how they share the gospel out of their own experience within
their social networks, but we don't control this from the center. How they
do what they do depends on the people in their house churches and 5-5-5
networks. They discover how to do it along the way, and those of us who
are more experienced are always finding that new disciples discover new
and sometimes even surprising ways that people live out the gospel in the
movement.

---

4 Brafman and Beckstrom, 19–20.

5 Brafman and Beckstrom, 35.

6 Sessoms, *Leading with Story*, 36–37.

Rethinking How We Lead

Christian leaders often adopt leadership patterns that have been developed in the business world without thinking through whether they are appropriate for the work in God's kingdom. For instance, in a command-and-control church system, the people are organized into a pyramid, reflecting what is found in most companies. When we apply this structure to the church, we might imagine it this way:

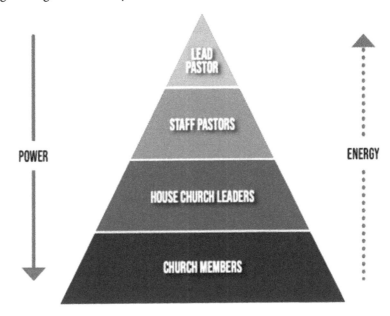

At the top, the boss is responsible for setting the vision and strategy for the church, which means that vision and strategy is limited to a few exclusive leaders who sit at the top with the senior pastor. The rest of the people are merely workers who get the boss's vision done. Rick Sessoms writes about this model of leadership, saying it communicates that one progresses in the realm of Christ's work as they rise to higher levels of rank in the system. The workers (church members) exist at a lower status and therefore they must be less committed to God's work. In addition, Rick argues that such a model of leadership equates leadership with power and authority rather than servitude and sacrifice.[7]

The development of such a model of leadership has a long history in business management. During the industrial revolution, key industries began to identify management patterns that would get more production out

---

7   Sessoms, 131.

of fewer people. Efficiency and effectiveness became the way to make more money. Sadly, many in the church have adopted these principles to increase their results.

Donald McGregor, an MIT management professor, identified the assumptions made by leaders who operate within the common pyramid. These assumptions include:

- The average person dislikes work and will avoid it if possible.
- People lack motivation and innovation, and are not goal-oriented; therefore, control and threats must be used to pressure them into action.
- The average person prefers to be directed and dislikes taking responsibility.
- Tough management is required if an organization wants to reach its goals; therefore, firmness and micromanagement are frequently necessary.
- The average person needs direction more than development.
- People depend on the intelligence of leaders.[8]

As I reflect on my work with pastors and church leaders in the many countries in which I have traveled, it is clear to me that these ideas have infiltrated the cultures of many churches around the world. Pastors' leadership assumptions about their people often dictate that they must operate at the top of a leadership pyramid. If we try to build a movement based on these ideas, we will eventually find that we're frustrated, and the movement will not have sustainable multiplication dynamics built into the DNA of the new converts.

Like most top-down organizations, motivation and authority flows from the top, leaving the largest group of people, which I call the "grassroots people," able to do only what the top gives them permission to do. This is the key obstacle to both the freedom of the Holy Spirit to work as he wills among the grassroots people and the Spirit-led personal drive within the grassroots people to engage freely with God and find the energy to do his good works.

In chapter 1, I introduced the parable of the mustard seed and how this illustrates the way that kingdom movements expand, beginning as something that is small and inconsequential and expanding to something large and significant. On the heels of that parable, Jesus told the parable of the yeast: "The kingdom of heaven is like yeast that a woman took and mixed into about sixty pounds of flour until it worked all through the dough" (Matt 13:33). This living yeast does not invade the flour because it has a head that is

---

8 Sessoms, 132.

commanding it to do so. It does it because that is just how yeast operates. This is how God's kingdom expands, if we will have eyes to see and ears to hear, if we will let go of our expectations of how we think God's people should be organized.

A Catalyst

Instead of a command-and-control leader that stands at the top of a pyramid, movements best flourish with the guidance of a leader who acts as a catalyst of circles. The Apostle Paul was the consummate catalyst of decentralized organizational life. He saw himself as a leader who fostered a way of organizing the church where the people of God were free to hear and obey the leading of the Spirit in their setting, without the need to have him present to tell them what to do. In other words, he generated starfish spaces that possessed the kingdom DNA and thereby could replicate on their own.

Donald McGregor also discovered a distinct set of assumptions made by leaders who want to go against the flow of the leadership pyramid. They are:

- People view work as a natural part of their lives.
- The average person is internally motivated to reach objectives to which he or she is committed.
- People will pursue common goals when they are properly encouraged.
- People will seek and accept responsibility under favorable conditions.
- People have the capacity to be innovative in solving problems.
- People are independently intelligent and will excel when trusted to.[9]

> The Apostle Paul was the consummate catalyst of decentralized organizational life.

These assumptions open the door for leaders to serve as catalysts rather than bosses. No man was ever meant to be the head of the church, because Christ is the head of God's body (Col 1:18). Movement catalysts foster the expanding work of the Spirit that trusts how Christ leads the church. In *The Starfish and the Spider*, Brafman and Beckstrom identify key traits of catalysts. Our experience aligns with theirs, and therefore I have adapted their list to fit movement work.

- Whereas a boss who sits at the top, a catalyst is a peer who walks alongside.
- Whereas a boss operates in command and in control, a catalyst teaches his people to trust in the Spirit and the Word, which abide in God's people.

---

9 Sessoms, 133.

- Whereas a boss makes decisions according to rational evaluation, a catalyst understands how to listen to the Spirit and teaches others to do the same.
- Whereas a boss leads through power, a catalyst inspires obedience to the Word of God and connects people to God's Word.
- Whereas a boss directs, a catalyst collaborates.
- Whereas a boss is in the spotlight, a catalyst works behind the scenes through his people at all levels.
- Whereas a boss maintains order in order to ensure the future of the organization, a catalyst embraces decentralization because he trusts the Lord to lead his people.
- Whereas a boss organizes to set up an impersonal structure, a catalyst only works through organically built relational structures.

One of the ways that we seek to elevate the importance of catalytic thinking is publicly viewed when we hold gatherings for training. We often promote the lower-level leaders, normally simple church leaders, and give them opportunities to speak. We limit the public exposure of our more senior leaders and try to give the platform to those leading in the most common positions.

In one meeting, when a 5-5-5 leader was speaking, the room erupted in a roar like we hear at a championship football game. I asked a brother what the reason was, and he said that this man speaking was someone that the audience totally identified with: a simple brother who loved the Lord and was allowed to speak. He noted that in the majority religion no one was ever allowed to speak who wasn't thoroughly trained and a skillful presenter, holding a high position in the organization.

His peers see that this movement is giving away ownership of the movement to those who are doing the work at the grassroots level.

We believe that Jesus flipped human ways on their head when he taught leaders to be the greatest servant of all, not the greatest speaker or teacher of all. Many things are happening when a leader who is not great according to cultural standards is elevated because he is faithful to God. His peers see that this movement is giving away ownership of the movement to those who are doing the work at the grassroots level. For the first time in their lives, these passionate men and women of God have the opportunity to exercise their leadership abilities and invest their lives in reaching those outside the faith with the gospel and then making disciples who make disciples.

A Hybrid System

Few purely decentralized organizations exist. Many are centralized, as they are driven by the leadership of the center while incorporating aspects of decentralization for the work centers where decentralization is appropriate. Others are decentralized in nature, but they run a few aspects of their work from within a well-defined structure. We might imagine such hybrid organizations along a spectrum from low to high decentralization. An organization must determine the decentralization "sweet spot" that fits the needs of its aims.

 Replication is a key element of movements that move, so our training is reproduced in a way that empowers the participants and is easily transferrable through the entire system.

In our case, our network of house churches is decentralized in the way that the churches operate. However, some functions do require a degree of centralization. For instance, we centralize our training development and yet it is given to our leaders to find the most important topics and use their own creativity in sharing it, giving ownership and authority, which is the decentralization of the training. Replication is a key element of movements that move, so our training is reproduced in a way that empowers the participants and is easily transferrable through the entire system. In addition, we collect and distribute relief funding in a centralized way. We ask the large number of local house churches to give a small amount weekly to a centralized account, which may be matched by outside funding, and then the distribution of funds in times of crisis is handled equitably to those in need. In both examples, centralization cooperates with the decentralization rather than competes with it.

Finally, the leadership that oversees what we call 5-5-5 networks is centralized, as the 5-5-5 leader serves as the "pastor," but it is a decentralized system because of the way that the growth works through new converts reaching five people each. The leader of the network challenges the new disciples to reach five people in their sphere of influence with the saving message of Christ. The new believers follow what they have learned and experienced with the guidance of the Spirit and do what they are led to do. The 5-5-5 leader operates as a catalyst, making a way for this work of the Holy Spirit.

The 5-5-5 System

We catalyze decentralization in our movement through a specific system that we call 5-5-5. The basic idea is quite simple, but to understand how it works you must imagine it from the grassroots level, not as an organization that is set up from the point of view of movement leaders. When new believers are baptized, we immediately ask them to begin sharing their testimony about what Jesus has done in their lives, with the goal of leading five of their family members and friends to Christ and then baptizing them. Every new believer, depicted in the center of the diagram below, is empowered to minister and draw five others to Christ. As the new Christians do this, they are operating as disciple-makers, not merely as disciples.

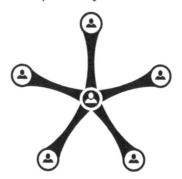

Subsequently, each new believer helps these five brand new Christians reach five persons and then baptize them when they come to faith. Notice in the diagram below the circular nature of what occurs. And no one is at the top.

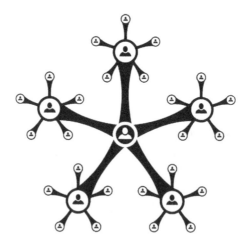

As this next generation of 25 new believers are being brought to Christ and baptized, each one is likewise challenged to reach 5 people, resulting in another 125 individuals who respond to the gospel and become disciple-makers. In this simple way, each initial person becomes an evangelist, mentor, and equipper for 5 persons, who in turn do the same for 5 new converts each, who repeat the process for another 25 persons. Thus an organic network of disciple-makers is born.

Some of these new networks don't stop at three generations, but continue multiplying far beyond. We have observed that we don't have to recruit house-church leaders, because the house churches are formed organically and the new leaders are eager to serve. House churches are a by-product of this decentralized way of operating. We don't think about strategies for starting house churches. Instead, we focus on empowering the principle of 5-5-5, and when there are enough people to meet as a house church, a new one is birthed. In each network of 155 baptized believers, there are about 20 to 25 house churches. The diagram below depicts a completed 5-5-5 network.

We focus on reaching the fathers of families first, and as a result most often whole families come to Christ and two families form a house church. The 5-5-5 network leader, as expected, becomes the support person, or pastor, of this group of house churches that he has mentored and coached into existence. Ownership of the ministry is not an issue. Everyone knows who has laid down their lives, taught and baptized, mentored and supported people through persecution and trials for the sake of the gospel.

However, there is a danger of this 5-5-5 network leader seeing himself as the boss within a centralized system. We are all tempted by the allure of being in charge. Consequently, we have sought to foster decentralization even further. We ask each 5-5-5 network leader to partner with four other 5-5-5 networks so that they can work together to oversee the five 5-5-5 networks. We have found that no one person can do this work alone. Network leaders need to meet together to support, challenge, and help each other.

They work at problem-solving, they strategize together, and they hold each other accountable. What a great way to foster humility, as leaders grow in their capacity for the Spirit to move through them. These leaders are called "Servants," and they choose a "Chief Servant" from among themselves to help guide the church; and that person only serves for one year before rotating out. The leaders can opt to bring an effective Chief Servant back for another tenure.

We call a network of five 5-5-5 networks a Village Church, or Neighborhood Church. Visually, it might look something like this:

Again, notice the viral, circular way that this operates. To be clear, these Village Churches do not meet in large groups. This is simply not possible. First, such a group would be far too large to function well in a group culture. Such meetings are not practical in the cultures where our movements are multiplying. In addition, meeting in such large groups would open the door to additional persecution. The Village Churches are also part of what will become an expanded basis for governance, which we will call Regional Churches.

We'll save this level of a decentralized leadership discussion for another time, but they are developed so that these Regional Churches can support the viral, decentralized work of the Spirit that is occurring at the grassroots level.

In other words, the growth of our movements occurs at the base level of the development of a 5-5-5 network. As soon as we think in terms of something larger than that, we are becoming unnecessarily centralized.

Conclusion

A few years ago I was in a training meeting with some of our 5-5-5 network leaders. I invited a friend, one of the initial movement innovators of movement strategies, to participate. In our sharing, we met a twenty-three-year-old man who had catalyzed five different 5-5-5 networks. This means that his ministry had influenced 750–800 people to follow Christ. He developed his network of house churches while continuing to earn his living as a factory worker. This man possesses the kingdom starfish DNA, and he was passing it on to others who are spawning new networks.

What struck me that day is the fact that this young man owned this vision and work. He didn't see his ministry as a subset of my ministry, as the original initiator of the movement, or as a subset of any of the local leaders with whom he works. This was his ministry to do, and he was releasing others to do likewise. We just listened to how he was being used by the Spirit. He knows what he is doing; and he had no need for our "expertise," as he was the true expert in his local context. The Spirit is at work in him, and in so many thousands of others like him.

Chapter 9

Leadership Best Practice #3: Learning Communities Develop New Leaders

Introduction

Asad looked around the small family room in his house while six house church leaders arrived and sat together on a Tuesday night after a long day of work. Three of them were farmers and the other three worked in a small factory. Rashid had been leading his house church for about a year, and he had already helped three other people start their own. He was well on his way to developing a 5-5-5 network. Moshin and Rayan had been leading a house church for a few months and were needing extra support because they had been experiencing some persecution. Sajid had only been a Christian disciple for about three weeks and had already led his entire family to Christ. They had started meeting together for worship in Sajid's home.

Asad had been praying for these men by name all afternoon, praying that the Spirit would minister to each one while they met.

We call such a meeting a Learning Community, or LC. It is a group of house church leaders who gather regularly—usually once or twice per month—for training and mutual support. During Asad's meeting, each leader talked about what he was facing, and extra time was spent discussing how the group could support the house churches that were facing persecution. Sajid raised questions about what to discuss in his newly formed house church. Rashid shared how he led a house church as a new Christian a year ago and the fears that he faced.

Asad led the group in a house-church Bible study provided by the movement leaders. They studied a Scripture story with questions that promoted practical application in their daily lives. A couple of key Bible verses were focused on, and everyone in the LC was encouraged to memorize them. Then they talked about how the Spirit was leading them to put those Scriptures into action. This led to a conversation about how this discussion could be repeated in the house churches.

We have thousands of these Learning Communities meeting on a regular basis. Without a doubt, this systemic element is the most significant strategic piece in our system. Learning Communities are the structural element that serves as the conduit for the life of the Spirit to flow to and through the house churches. If you were to identity one structural element that develops leadership in our movement, this is it. Without Learning Communities, our movement would not be where it is today. These LCs facilitate peer learning and promote community, obedience-based discipleship, and Jesus's culture of serving, along with providing tremendous support for everyday life in a sometimes-hostile environment. Leadership development is the greatest challenge for a massive movement, so these LCs are fundamental to our success.

> Leaders learn through concrete experience and then replicate what they have learned with others.

Learning Communities are venues of training through modeling. Leaders learn through concrete experience and then replicate what they have learned with others. The key thought here is *concrete*. These communities are relationally-based groups in which people discover what it means to lead others in general and to lead a house church in particular, as they continually observe the 5-5-5 leader who is leading their group. Life on life. The love of Jesus flows. Jesus's teachings and instructions from the Gospels are discussed. People tell stories and relate their challenges in local, colloquial fashion.

This isn't formal training, but rather the community of Christ functioning in forms that are contextually comfortable. Jesus's sacrifice has brought the joy of eternal life. Replacing the law of Islam, or the fear-based Hindu efforts to appease gods, with the love of Jesus in their hearts changes everything, but it doesn't change their cultural norms. We see people with an Islamic or Hindu past, living as disciple-makers of Jesus Christ in an Islamic or Hindu culture.

Training Mistakes

Before going deeper into how Learning Communities operate, I want to highlight some common training mistakes that people make as they pursue movement work.

The first mistake occurs when house-church leaders are released to go it alone. No leader—even the most gifted of us—is meant to lead alone. All leaders need training and support as they serve others. In addition, none of us ever outgrows the need to grow in the grace of God and in the Word. As I stated in chapter 6, our research shows that leaders require ongoing, continuous training as they serve in a movement. Training in the Word of God is imperative. These LCs experience the highly contextualized biblical training developed by the movement leaders in a context that oral learners can absorb and repeat. We encourage our leaders to memorize Scripture that is empowering, encouraging, and life-giving. Without the Word, we cannot grow.

> Learning Communities provide just-in-time training that can be repeated immediately in their context.

A second commonly made mistake is engaging in leadership training before someone is leading. Sometimes church leaders are taught in the "just-in-case" model of training, where they receive a lot of information that they may someday need to know. In a worst-case scenario, leaders are sometimes removed from their context, often for months or even years, and sent to a seminary or Bible-school environment. When they return to their former life, the adjustment is typically quite challenging, and adapting their learning to their old context is even more difficult. In terms of movement growth, this model of training will result in failure and an unsustainable movement for many reasons, as addressed in previous chapters. Instead, our Learning Communities provide just-in-time training that can be repeated immediately in their context.

Also, with the network of leaders meeting in a Learning Community, even the newly minted house-church leaders will have more experienced leaders to lean on as they learn the process and the Word. Peer learning and peer mentoring means that those in your LC are from your culture and think like you do, and yet have put on Christ and are a few weeks or months ahead of you in the process of change in this new life in Jesus.

A third common mistake is the use of training that focuses on theoretical information. Oral learners primarily want and need concrete thinking and training. They need to learn stories and behaviors that they can live out in their daily lives. To do this, we simply present a passage from the Bible and have them discuss some basic questions, such as "What does this passage teach us about God?" "What does it teach us about humans?" and "Is there an instruction to be obeyed?" These questions are similar to DBS questions, however we also supply study guides to help our people discuss and obey biblical truths.

We focus on passages in the Bible related to the stories and teachings of Christ: how he lived and interacted with his disciples and others. Stories are the key to everything. In the Learning Community, neophytes learn the biblical stories that apply to their lives and context. The works of the Spirit, the gifts of the Spirit, the healings that they see happen before their eyes, are passed from one person to another and one Learning Community to another. Everyone is sharing their faith and working to reach five. This common goal gives our people much to share with each other about what God is blessing, how to deal with challenges, and methods of sharing Christ that fit the context.

Another mistake made by those who are developing leadership training is that they develop content that depends on experts to be taught well. Such experts may have received specialized training about theological issues founded on abstract thinking. However, practically speaking, when such experts are required to train leaders, like all of us, they only know how to pass on content in the way that they were taught, which may have been in a classroom setting. The classroom is not available, nor desired, as we use home environments and sit in a circle facing each other.

> The best way to learn is to teach others what you have learned.

Also, concrete thinking dominates oral cultures, so new converts are typically lost when we approach them with complex, abstract thinking. As you will see in the next chapter, as I discuss various aspects of adult education, the best way to learn is through practical, hands-on, experiential growth. Training that depends upon an expert nullifies the primary power of communal learning through dialogue and storytelling.

A fifth critical mistake is made when the training is developed in such a way that it cannot be easily repeated by those who have been trained. The best way to learn is to teach others what you have learned. Research has proven that repeating training in exactly the same way you learned it is most effective. Process is everything. However, if the way that you received the training cannot be easily replicated, then it will not be highly transferrable. A simple illustration of this is an outsider who brings in a PowerPoint presentation for his teaching. Will all the participants receive a copy and have the equipment and technological skill to teach it, in just the way that they learned it? Our training is delivered so that others can transfer the content and experience in the same way. In fact, this point is so crucial, I have dedicated chapter 13 to it.

These five mistakes are all rooted in one thing: they all assume a classroom approach to training, in which trainees receive information without conversation, context, and story. Usually this occurs as people sit in rows, with each student sitting alone listening to a teacher or other expert telling them how to think and behave. The educational system in many cultures strongly discourages questions and independent thinking. Rote memorization is the path to success, and comparative, analytical thinking is discouraged. In contrast, Learning Communities are designed so that training occurs in circles, where leaders are actively learning together. They are doing together what they will repeat with others, and the Word of God is able to instruct, inspire, and challenge everyone. Because this is experiential learning, almost everything that occurs in the Learning Community can be repeated in a house church.

Characteristics of Learning Communities

When I initially explored practical ways to live out the "Principle of Continual Training," which I explained in *Movements That Move*, I studied *Professional Learning Communities at Work*, by Richard DuFour and Robert Eaker. This book addresses how schools can be enhanced as teachers and administrators meet together in Learning Communities, as opposed to simply doing the work of teaching in isolation. Their research served as a launchpad for our work. The authors identify six characteristics of Learning Communities that apply both to a school setting as well as that of a movement system.[1]

1. **Shared mission, vision, and values.** Mission identifies why we exist. Vision states what we hope to become. And values name how we behave in order to make our shared vision a reality. These must be clear for all involved. In our situation, this is not only clear, but simple. Our movement exists because of the command of Christ to make disciple-makers, based on his sacrificial love for us demonstrated on the cross. Our vision is to disciple people to a life of obedient faith in Jesus Christ and, through the 5-5-5 networking system, to make disciple-makers. Our values are focused on obedience to the teachings of Jesus Christ, and our behaviors focus on helping our people share what Christ has done in their lives with five individuals in their social network. Of course, a lifetime of personal growth in our relationships with Christ and his followers awaits us; but in order to keep it simple, this is what everyone in the movement is about.

2. **Collective inquiry.** When training occurs in a group, there is space for open interaction and learning together. Everyone brings their questions and challenges to the group, and the answers come through a variety of voices. New believers and house-church leaders are helped by experienced leaders.

1 DuFour and Eaker, *Professional Learning Communities at Work*, 25–29.

3. **Collaborative teams.** The Learning Community leader is a facilitator of mutual learning, as each Learning Community works together to address problems in the believing community, learn about the teachings of the Bible, and learn how to address difficulties that families face in the larger community.

4. **Action and Obedience.** Members of Learning Communities are focused on getting involved in what God is doing in real life as they interact with their families, friends, and neighbors. Dufour and Eaker note that participants in Learning Communities "recognize that learning always occurs in the context of taking action, and they believe engagement and experience are the most effective teachers."[2]

   This is not theoretical learning that they might need at some point in the future. It is founded upon action and obedience. They learn, and then they act—in compliance with Jesus's words that "Anyone who loves me will obey my teaching" (John 14:23). This action and obedience is often lived out in compassionate outreach to hurting neighbors, both disciples of Jesus and others.

5. **Continuous improvement.** This training school is not one from which leaders graduate. It represents a lifelong learning journey with God together. As I will explain below, those who lead multiple Learning Communities, because they have fostered many 5-5-5 networks, are also supported within a Learning Community. No one is left to lead alone.

6. **Results orientation.** We have a clear purpose in our movement. We aim to share the gospel with as many people as possible and to make disciple-makers. This drives all that we do, and the Learning Community is a space where leaders can grow in their capacity for this purpose.

All six of these characteristics are accomplished as an LC meets in a group, just as they would be in their house church. They learn by doing. And the more they do it, the more the process naturally replicates itself.

Learning Communities in the Bible

When we peruse the pages of the Scriptures, we are hard-pressed to find anything directly related to the specific structure that we have developed. However, the principle of leaders teaching, modeling, and encouraging other leaders in a group context pervades the Bible. For the most part, we must

---

2 DuFour and Eaker, 27.

look indirectly at the overall narrative to see this happening, as this kind of training is occurring just beneath the surface. Only in a few places do we find direct instructions that relate.

One direct reference is found in 2 Timothy 2:2, where Paul wrote to Timothy, a young church leader he had been mentoring: "The things you have heard me say in the presence of many witnesses entrust to reliable people who will also be qualified to teach others." Paul instructed Timothy to share that which Paul had shared with him: giving it away to others who in turn would be able to give it away. Leaders pass on what they have received to other leaders who then, in turn, can give it away. This is the way of God's kingdom. It's never about one person being able to do more ministry directly to more people. God's kingdom multiplies as more and more leaders are trained.

> Paul modeled through relationships. This can be surmised when we consider that this is how he received his own training: by walking with Barnabas in life-on-life mentoring.

Even more importantly, it's not merely what Paul said, but how he said it, that reveals the importance of learning in this way. Paul modeled through relationships. This can be surmised when we consider that this is how he received his own training: by walking with Barnabas in life-on-life mentoring. Paul invested in Timothy in the same way that Barnabas had invested in him. Imagine how Paul worked with Mark, Luke, Lydia, Titus, Pricilla and Aquilla, along with many others. He was not simply leading meetings with his leaders or teaching them in a classroom. He was doing ministry alongside them; and more importantly, they were doing ministry alongside each other. This was life lived together: sailing the waters of the Mediterranean and walking the roads of the region; fasting, praying, dealing with opposition, and finding joy and strength in each other and the Holy Spirit.

In our context, the formal meeting of a Learning Community is merely a way to facilitate relational training. While we don't have any direct historical evidence that leaders of house churches met together on a regular basis during the first century, it is likely that they did, simply because these churches were connected. And as a minority religion—often viewed as a cult during this time—facing persecution, they needed the support of each other, as well as senior leaders like Paul and Timothy.

In the same way, in times of financial crisis our Learning Communities band together to address financial needs in their house churches, in their 5-5-5 network and in the movement at large. Recently our 5-5-5 networks raised $30,000 to help widows in their villages, the "least of these" in their communities. Funds are raised for relief during seasonal flooding, for food during COVID, for whatever the needs are. Times of fasting and prayer are initiated by the LCs to pray together for those who are sick. The LCs occasionally go together to confront an Imam or other leaders who may be persecuting our people. When a group shows up at the home of a persecutor, sharing the love of Jesus and is able to demonstrate their knowledge about the constitutional freedom of religion, most often the persecution stops immediately, and occasionally the persecutor joins the ranks of the disciples.

Another Scripture passage where we might infer that something like Learning Communities exists is Exodus 18. Here Jethro tells his son-in-law, Moses, that he should not lead every person in Israel directly, but he should appoint leaders over tens, fifties, hundreds, and thousands.

> Moses' father-in-law replied, "What you are doing is not good. You and these people who come to you will only wear yourselves out. The work is too heavy for you; you cannot handle it alone. Listen now to me and I will give you some advice, and may God be with you. You must be the people's representative before God and bring their disputes to him. Teach them his decrees and instructions, and show them the way they are to live and how they are to behave. But select capable men from all the people—men who fear God, trustworthy men who hate dishonest gain—and appoint them as officials over thousands, hundreds, fifties and tens. Have them serve as judges for the people at all times, but have them bring every difficult case to you; the simple cases they can decide themselves. That will make your load lighter, because they will share it with you. If you do this and God so commands, you will be able to stand the strain, and all these people will go home satisfied."
>
> Moses listened to his father-in-law and did everything he said. He chose capable men from all Israel and made them leaders of the people, officials over thousands, hundreds, fifties and tens. They served as judges for the people at all times. The difficult cases they brought to Moses, but the simple ones they decided themselves. – Exodus 18:17–26

Moses was trying to lead the people of Israel alone. Jethro told him that he needed to multiply himself in others so that all could be led effectively and Moses wouldn't burn out. In this way the people could be served "at all times" (verses 22, 26), instead of the limited times when Moses was available to the entire nation. Moses' father-in-law proposed a system whereby everyone could be cared for. This system of decentralizing leadership for Moses is the way we have established our movement. In order to achieve a broad-based decentralized system of governance and leadership, we must have a means of raising up leaders. Learning Communities is our answer.

Learning Communities and the 5-5-5 System: The Essential Structure to Developing New Leaders

In the previous chapter I introduced the 5-5-5 system, which catalyzes a decentralized movement. As I have mentioned, the Learning Communities are integral to this decentralization because they equip leaders to follow the leading of the Spirit and they build biblical knowledge and obedience in our disciples. We have found that we need different kinds of Learning Communities for the different levels within the 5-5-5 system. The first are grassroots Learning Communities comprised of one leader from each of six to ten house churches.

A typical 5-5-5 network will have twenty to twenty-five house churches, so each network might have two to four of these LC small-group meetings each month. These are the primary Learning Communities, as they are closest to the front lines of movement development and also serve to build the community of a network. The 5-5-5 leaders are the facilitators of these Learning Communities, of which we have thousands.

> We need different kinds of Learning Communities for the different levels within the 5-5-5 system.

Generally, the people in these gatherings know each other well, since the organic systems of conversion growth focus on the social networks of friends and family members. All have made a radical commitment to be a disciple of Jesus and to make disciple-makers, so bonding is strong and immediate. Whatever persecution they have experienced normally bakes in their commitments to Christ and each other.

The second level of LCs is for the 5-5-5 leaders who have started and completed a 5-5-5 network. Just to restate the context, these men and women have won five friends or family to Christ, baptized them, then coached and mentored them to do the same through two more generations and a total of 155 people who become disciples. This level of Learning Community for these 5-5-5 leaders occurs monthly and is geographically organized. At this point, there are more than ten thousand 5-5-5 leaders involved.

There are additional levels of LCs for those selected by their peers to help facilitate the movement's more centralized activities based on the governance model of the nation. In the US we might have city, county, state, and regional leaders. Whatever the governance norm for the nation where we have planted and cultivated these 5-5-5 movements, they select leaders who have proven faithful to the gospel and effective in developing 5-5-5 networks. Although the complexity is too difficult to explore in this book, there are additional levels of functioning LCs that help develop and pass down training and other functional issues. Training is passed down from one level of LC to another until, finally, the house churches are impacted.

When these Learning Communities meet, they worship together, pray for each other's personal needs, study the Bible in a conversational way, receive training, discuss challenges related to persecution or the need for flood or food relief, and generally solve problems. In these highly relational gatherings, deep bonds are forged between leaders as they share the burdens and joys of being God's servants. Through these relationships, we have found that there are natural outcomes from training and building community in small groups of leaders.

Learning Community Outcomes

In our context, Learning Communities are a natural fit because the social structure is group-oriented. Our people don't think about their lives within a Western, individualistic frame, but their identities are directly integrated into their families, neighbors, and friends. They think in terms of "us," not in terms of "me."

This is challenging to grasp in a Western context. The concept of *ubuntu* in the Xhosa culture in Africa illustrates this point of view. An anthropologist proposed a game to the kids in an African tribe. He put a basket full of fruit near a tree and told them that whoever got there first, could have the sweet fruits. When he gave them the signal to run, they all took one another's hands and ran together, and then they sat in a circle enjoying their treats. When the anthropologist asked them why they chose to run as a group when they might have gotten more fruit individually, one child spoke up and said, "*Ubuntu*—How can one of us be happy if all the other ones are sad?"

Learning Communities are a natural fit for group-oriented cultures because everyone wants to work together to see everyone advance and enjoy the fruit of God's kingdom. This is not about individual growth; it's about kingdom promotion through the entire group, which results in specific outcomes.

The first outcome is that Learning Communities connect the entire system of house churches. The house churches, therefore, are never left on their own. They are part of the momentum of a larger system, which supports the life of each house church. Some might think that the house churches are developed to support the larger movement or the vision of the leaders at the top. The opposite is the case. The larger system is designed to support the house churches, and the Learning Communities are the practical mechanism for facilitating that support.

> Learning Communities connect the entire system of house churches. The house churches, therefore, are never left on their own.

Secondly, Learning Communities help pass along biblical teaching and practical application of training through the entire 5-5-5 system. As I will demonstrate in the next chapter, the training that is provided in a Learning Community can be passed on to other Learning Communities and ultimately to the house churches. Both the content and the learning methods that disseminate that content is passed down through the system. Of course, sharing stories from the Word of God and then stories of the practical application of the teachings of Jesus Christ are foundational to communication and growth.

The most crucial outcomes of the Learning Community system is the support that is provided to the house churches. This is especially evident in a context that includes persecution. Salman listened to his group share about what they were facing. Nadeem talked about how his former Imam had paid his family a visit and was spreading rumors about him in the village. They were struggling as a house church, and he was wondering if the pressure from the Imam and their community would be too much to bear. After the meeting, the Learning Community walked to the home of the Imam and challenged him. The solidarity and support of eight disciples of Jesus caused him to back off, which has happened over and over.

I've heard such stories more times than I can count. Learning Communities undergird the life of the house churches, providing strength when there are challenges and helping to celebrate the victories. When persecutions stop the families from getting water from the village well, cut off schooling opportunities for the children, or ostracize individual Christians, the Learning Communities step in with practical assistance.

A final outcome is the healthy distribution of financial support to those in house churches. The Learning Community is a conduit where needs are communicated to leaders and funds go to the places of need, without having to develop extensive administrative mechanisms. I will address this further in chapter 12.

Conclusion

Kashif began leading his house church after he led his wife and her parents to Christ, and simultaneously he started attending the Learning Community that Sameer led. He worked with Sameer at a factory, and was blessed to lead Kashif to Christ. They often rode the bus together after work, and they would talk about the Bible and pray together. Kashif had many questions about Jesus and how to share the joy of his salvation with others.

Kashif watched how Sameer led the Learning Community meetings, and he would repeat what he learned there in his own house church. Now Kashif guides a 5-5-5 network and leads a Learning Community in which all the members lead their own Learning Community. And all of this developed within eighteen months. It's a simple process of life on life, without formal education to interfere; and it works much like the church life found in the book of Acts.

Chapter 10

Leadership Best Practice #4: Foster Obedience-Based Discipleship

Introduction

Basan, a farmer in a rural community, grew up in a Muslim family, as do millions in Southeast Asia. He attended the local mosque periodically, but he didn't know much about the Quran, as he had never been taught to read well. He just trusted what the Imam told him. During the time farmers wait for their crops to grow and thus have less work to do, Basan heard a neighbor, Fairuz, tell stories about Isa and how the Koran actually talked about him. At first Basan scoffed, but Fairuz talked about eternal life and how, after we die, we can live with God forever, something that Basan had not heard in the teachings of Islam. After more conversations, especially when he heard how Fairuz had been healed after being prayed for in the name of Isa, Basan believed and was baptized.

Basan started attending the house church that met in Fairuz's home and told his wife, Aamirah, about Isa. She struggled with his decision because her father was an Imam, and she did not want to experience rejection from her family. But Basan sensed that something new was occurring in his life that he could not deny, so he continued in his discipleship. He experienced persecution, as more family members challenged him and the local Imam put pressure on him to reject Isa.

During harvest time, other farmers did not help Basan bring in his crops. When their son became ill, so ill that it looked like he was going to die, Basan's wife became so desperate that she told Basan to pray in the name of Isa. Others from the house church came and prayed for him, and he miraculously recovered overnight. When she saw this miracle, she gave her life to Isa.

Within a year Basan not only led his family to Christ and began mentoring them—just as he had been mentored by Fauruz—but also six other families believed and were baptized. Two families met in his home, and the others met in their own homes, as house churches. They joined in the 5-5-5 network that Basan began, and each led five to Christ and personally baptized them, challenging them to lead five of their friends and family members to eternal life in Isa, meeting together regularly.

 > New house churches are a by-product of disciples making disciples. A Jesus movement is not a "church-planting movement," but a movement of disciples making disciples.

Basan's experience is a typical story of a typical disciple. Basan is a disciple who is making disciples. A Jesus movement is a movement of disciples who invest in other people so that they might make disciples. New house churches are a by-product of disciples making disciples. A Jesus movement is not a "church-planting movement," but a movement of disciples making disciples. We are mobilizing disciples to share their faith with people already in their social networks, and then these disciples are forming churches.

Fairuz invited Basan into a specific form of discipleship, one commonly called obedience-based discipleship. Across the board, in all the movements that have continued to experience kingdom multiplication of Jesus disciple-makers, obedience-based discipleship is the standard. In other words, they take seriously that the Great Commission of Jesus is not about making converts but about making disciples who make disciples, teaching them to obey Christ's teachings.

Obedience

In the Bible, there is a common sentence structure in which a statement is made and then a follow-up statement or clause expounds upon it. This is called parallelism, and we often miss it because we tend to read each part separately instead of seeing how the second part fleshes out the first. For example, John 3:36 in the New American Standard Bible (NASB) reads, "The one who believes in the Son has eternal life; but the one who does not obey the Son will not see life, but the wrath of God remains on him." Belief, in this passage, is defined by the second part of the verse where we read about the need to "obey the Son." Belief in the first part is defined by the second part.

In the Great Commission, Jesus commands us to "make disciples of all nations." We are not left to ourselves to define what it means to make disciples, because there is a follow-up sentence that explains what disciple-making looks like. Let's look at Jesus's words at the end of Matthew more closely:

> Therefore go and make disciples of all nations, baptizing them in the name
> of the Father and of the Son and of the Holy Spirit, and teaching them to

obey everything I have commanded you. And surely I am with you always, to the very end of the age. – Matthew 28:19–20

First, making disciples involves baptism in the name of the Father, the Son, and the Holy Spirit. This is a significant act, both in the context of first-century Christianity and in modern-day Jesus movements. Often those of us who have grown up in Western Christianity miss this because being baptized is simply a common act that has very few social ramifications. But in the first century it was a public announcement whereby believers acted out their allegiance. It signified that the new disciple had crossed a line from one group to another. The same is true today. Individuals in a Muslim society can say that they believe in Jesus with few repercussions, but to be baptized is another thing altogether. It is a confession that they have moved into a whole new social belonging. It is an action that signifies they have become a committed member of another faith, which often leads to persecution and shunning.

Second, making disciples involves "teaching them to obey" everything that Jesus taught his first disciples. Discipleship is directly connected to living out the way of Jesus, as we see throughout the stories recorded in the book of Acts. Nowhere do we find evidence of the early church simply trying to make converts. They aimed at being followers of Jesus who were seeking to help others become followers of Jesus. Nominal, spectator Christianity, while prevalent in many churches today, was not even an option for disciples in the first three centuries. To believe in Christ was to obey, to live in a way that reflects the teachings of Christ, and it often meant persecution of various types and even dying for their beliefs.

Obedience-based discipleship drives the action of kingdom movements because this way of being God's people ensures that God's ways are the norm. This stands in contrast to a way of being God's people that is rooted in knowledge-based discipleship. The following offers a brief comparison of the two.

	Knowledge-Based	Obedience-Based
Focus	Information	Action
Timeline	Years	Immediate
Candidates	Few	All
Format	Teaching/Listening	Dialogue
Setting	Classroom	Relationships/Mentoring
Accountability Level	Low	High
Method	Memorization of Facts	Experimentation

> The established churches in the West have become experts in knowledge-based discipleship, which is based on packaged curriculum, books, and classes that dispense information.

Movement experts David and Paul Watson write, "In reality, we [church leaders] have been teaching knowledge not obedience. Most people already know what they are supposed to do, but they choose not to do it."[1] The established churches in the West have become experts in knowledge-based discipleship, which is based on packaged curriculum, books, and classes that dispense information. This is discipleship founded on the assumption that if people learn the right information, they will change how they live.

This is totally off the mark because transformation requires obedience. We can know information, but when we don't act on it, then we become Pharisaical. First John 2:4 says, "The one who says, 'I have come to know Him,' and does not keep His commandments, is a liar, and the truth is not in him" (NASB). In this knowledge-based model of discipleship, accountability is low because the information itself should do the work, if people learn the facts correctly. Normally it does not.

Jerry Trousdale writes about this in his book, *The Kingdom Unleashed*.

> Many Christians in the Global North seem to think that transformation is a purely internal matter, accomplished through studying the Scriptures and perhaps through prayer. This reflects the knowledge-based model of discipleship common in Global North evangelicalism. We certainly don't intend to downplay the importance of studying and meditating on Scriptures—but it is equally important to obey it. When Jesus discusses the last judgment, He does not tell us that He will judge us based on whether we pass a Scripture quiz; He tells us He judges based on how we live our life.[2]

Obedience-based discipleship takes a different approach. The Bible is still crucial, but it is not merely a source of information. It is a guide for action for all, as all are invited into conversations about what it means to follow Jesus in the daily realities that they face. This is the nature of what it means to follow Christ. Jesus made this clear when he said, "If you love me, you will obey my commandments" (John 14:15 GNT).

Our love for God is more than a feeling that we experience; it plays out in the way we act, the way that we work out our faith. And this obedience causes us to grow in our knowledge of God's love. It is exhilarating to see Christians who have only known Jesus for months grow in their knowledge and love for

1   Watson and Watson, *Contagious Disciple Making*, 46.

2   Trousdale, *Kingdom Unleashed*, 317–18.

God because they have put their faith in action. They have tested what they believe through their obedience.

> We don't wait until Christians have achieved a "level of maturity," normally defined by acquiring knowledge, before we challenge them to obey.

Therefore, we emphasize immediate discipleship. We don't wait until Christians have achieved a "level of maturity," normally defined by acquiring knowledge, before we challenge them to obey. All Christians are disciples and disciple-makers, even those who are new to the faith. Immediate discipleship is crucial. Disciples make disciples not because they have become expert teachers but because they are walking with other disciples as a mentor, showing them the way to walk with Christ. And therefore the accountability is high, because they are deeply involved in each other's lives on a daily basis. Finally, they obey not because they have attained a specified level of knowledge. They learn as they go, as they take risks in their obedience, trusting God for what they don't fully understand. This is called "faith" in the New Testament.

Reach Five

We make immediate obedience-based discipleship concrete in the life of our movement. Newly baptized believers are challenged to identify people in their lives with whom they will share their newfound faith, with the goal of leading five to Christ. New converts from another religion are taught from the beginning that being a disciple-maker is the core of what it means to follow Jesus Christ. For us, this is the first and most important step. We must be careful not to overlook the potentially most effective and passionate missionaries on the earth, new converts. They have built-in social networks of families and friends who have known them all their lives and with whom they have influence and who are probably curious as to their life change. These unreached family and friends may fight against the newfound faith in Christ, but some may listen. Spirit-inspired testimonies from trusted relations have a significant impact. When trouble comes to their lives, as it does to us all, these family and friends may be open to prayer and the help given by God, who answers new converts' prayers.

All are called to obey immediately, and this practice is built into the DNA of the movement. Curtis Sergeant calls this kind of discipleship "Theopraxy," which he defines as

> a lifestyle that seeks to know Christ, to imitate him, to seek God's Kingdom, and to view everything in life from God's perspective. It requires a desire to live in total concord with and submission to his will, ways, purposes,

character, nature, desires, and thoughts. It is doing God's work, in God's way, in God's timing, by God's enablement.[3]

Theopraxy literally means "God practice," as it emphasizes not only the right things to do, but also the right way of doing them—that is, doing them in the power and the presence of God, who lives in our midst. This obedience flows out of our life with Christ, which points back to the practice we highlighted in chapter 7: "Depend upon the power of the Holy Spirit."

> Setting the goal for everyone to reach five makes obedience-based discipleship practical and tangible.

Setting the goal for everyone to reach five makes obedience-based discipleship practical and tangible. All are challenged. All are mentored. And all are invited to depend upon the presence and leading of the Spirit to reach five people.

The Bible and Obedience

This view of discipleship should not shock us, as obedience—not knowledge—pervades the Scriptures. Relationship with God always entails some form of obedience. This began in the Garden of Eden, where God walked with Adam and Eve in the cool of the evening. However, he didn't just relate to them; he instructed them to "Be fruitful and increase in number; fill the earth and subdue it. Rule over the fish in the sea and the birds in the sky and over every living creature that moves on the ground" (Gen 1:28).

In other words, he commanded them to multiply and partner with him in caring for the earth. This pattern continues throughout the Old Testament, as is exemplified by the Ten Commandments and the entire Torah. Obedience is directly tied to Israel's relationship with God.

Then, in the New Testament, Jesus taught us the two greatest commands: to love God and to love others. After washing the feet of the disciples, he told them that they should do likewise. Specifically, Jesus told his disciples,

> Now that I, your Lord and Teacher, have washed your feet, you also should wash one another's feet. I have set you an example that you should do as I have done for you. Very truly I tell you, no servant is greater than his master, nor is a messenger greater than the one who sent him. Now that you know these things, you will be blessed if you do them. —John 13:14–17

A biblical view of discipleship is manifest by doing what Jesus did, not through knowing information. This should not be a radical idea that is merely a movement principle. Obedience is basic to what it means to be Christ's disciple. Jesus was crystal clear when he said, "Anyone who loves me will obey my teaching" (John 14:23).

---

3 Sergeant, *The Only One*, xviii.

The Seeds of the Kingdom

Beyond the fact that discipleship is based in obedience within our movements, we have experienced how obedience leads to such radical transformation and produces movement fruit. This can be illustrated through the Parable of the Sower in Mark 4.

> "Listen! A farmer went out to sow his seed. As he was scattering the seed, some fell along the path, and the birds came and ate it up. Some fell on rocky places, where it did not have much soil. It sprang up quickly, because the soil was shallow. But when the sun came up, the plants were scorched, and they withered because they had no root. Other seed fell among thorns, which grew up and choked the plants, so that they did not bear grain. Still other seed fell on good soil. It came up, grew and produced a crop, some multiplying thirty, some sixty, some a hundred times."
>
> Then Jesus said, "Whoever has ears to hear, let them hear."
>
> When he was alone, the Twelve and the others around him asked him about the parables. He told them, "The secret of the kingdom of God has been given to you. But to those on the outside everything is said in parables so that,
>
>> "'they may be ever seeing but never perceiving,
>> and ever hearing but never understanding;
>> otherwise, they might turn and be forgiven!'"
>
> Then Jesus said to them, "Don't you understand this parable? How then will you understand any parable? The farmer sows the word. Some people are like seed along the path, where the word is sown. As soon as they hear it, Satan comes and takes away the word that was sown in them. Others, like seed sown on rocky places, hear the word and at once receive it with joy. But since they have no root, they last only a short time. When trouble or persecution comes because of the word, they quickly fall away. Still others, like seed sown among thorns, hear the word; but the worries of this life, the deceitfulness of wealth and the desires for other things come in and choke the word, making it unfruitful. Others, like seed sown on good soil, hear the word, accept it, and produce a crop—some thirty, some sixty, some a hundred times what was sown." —Mark 4:3–20

The seed (the Word of God) is sown in the good soil—people who respond in obedience as they hear the word, accept it, and produce a crop. But what is going on with this seed, the Word of God? This is part of the "secret" of the kingdom of God, as Jesus said in verse 11. The word secret here can also be translated as "mystery." There is a mystery going on with the seed, as we do not fully understand how a seed is planted in the ground and then turns into a plant that looks entirely different from that seed and then produces other seeds.

> The seed (the Word of God) is sown in the good soil—people who respond in obedience as they hear the word, accept it, and produce a crop.

That seed burrows down in the good soil and is nurtured there through the Word. As we mediate on the Word day and night (Psalm 1) our hearts are prepared for producing a new kind of fruit. Prayer, memorizing the Word, worship, fasting, meditation day and night, all contribute to nurturing the seed, as the seed transforms the human heart. However, to get from knowledge to transformation, something else must happen.

Nurturing the seed of God's Word alone is not enough. Obeying the Word becomes a significant change agent in the process. Obedience cracks open the outer shell of the seed, and allows the divine energy contained within to be released to transform the heart of the hearer. We know from Hebrews 4:12 that "the word of God is alive and active. Sharper than any double-edged sword, it penetrates even to dividing soul and spirit, joints and marrow." Jesus identifies himself as the Word in John 1:1, where the Bible says, "In the beginning was the Word, and the Word was with God, and the Word was God." So obedience to the Word is obeying Christ and releasing him to do his work in our hearts and lives. Without obedience, the seed lies dormant in the heart of man, its power to transform restricted and restrained by disobedience.

Obedience and the House-Church Meetings

Obedience-based discipleship is built into the most basic element of a movement, the gatherings in homes. We have developed a way of meeting that guides those who gather to talk about the Scripture and then to hear the challenge of the Spirit to respond to it. I have included a sample of the lesson on the next few pages.

We have built obedience into these lessons. For instance, each lesson provides time for the group to reflect on the homework from the previous week. In every case, this homework focuses on how they were being challenged by the Spirit to act upon the previous lesson. This is when the house-church members hold each other accountable to their commitments. In addition, the questions are designed to guide the group to talk about ways that they can put the Scripture into practice in their daily lives. And finally, each meeting leads to instructions regarding homework that is tied to the lesson.

This is not a Bible study. It is a Bible obedience guide that aims at helping the house churches understand and obey the Scripture passage that is being discussed.

Sample House-Church Lesson Foundations of the Christian Life Lesson 10: Meeting Needs, Blessing People

Main Idea: God calls us to give of our resources so that we can be a blessing to other people who are in need.

1. **Sing a Song**

2. **Opening Prayer**

3. **Everyone say out loud, one at a time, the Scripture memorized last week.**

   - *"In everything I did, I showed you that by this kind of hard work we must help the weak, remembering the words the Lord Jesus himself said: 'It is more blessed to give than to receive.'"* (Acts 20:35 NIV)

   - **Leader: Praise those who memorized the verse. Offer to help those who did not. Break into groups of two or three to practice the verse if necessary.**

4. **Homework**

   - **Leader: Before discussing this week's lesson, have everyone report on how they did on the homework from last week, listed below.**

   - **Homework:** Meet with someone this week and give them something that will be a blessing to them. Maybe they are in need financially. Maybe they need food. Maybe they need time with you as a friend. Maybe they need help with their field work or their house. Each person should ask the Holy Spirit to lead them in how you can give to someone else. Be prepared to share next week what the Lord had you do and how it was received by the person you blessed.

   - **Repeat out loud. Memorize for next week.**
     "At the present time your plenty will supply what they need, so that in turn their plenty will supply what you need. The goal is equality." *(2 Corinthians 8:14 NIV)*

   - **The Leader reads and repeats the verse, and the group says it together out loud, two times. Challenge the group to memorize it. Help them do so.**

5. **Teaching from the Bible**

6. **Leader: Share the following illustration to introduce the lesson.**

   - We know farmers work in cultivation. They plough land, plant seeds, and then collect crops. Every year farmers store some good seeds from the collected crops to plant next year. Seeds are like assets or resources to farmers. They can plant the seeds they saved up and have another crop next year. In the same way, if we store up money to be given to others in their time of need, we are preparing a crop of blessing for God's people in their time of need.

7. **Have someone read 2 Corinthians 8:13-15 out loud. The Leader summarizes the passage in their own words and lets the group add anything left out. Read the passage a second time, then discuss the questions below.**

   - According to this passage, what is the goal of our giving?

   - Are we to give, even if it causes us to be in need?

   - If we have more than we need for the day or the week, what are we to do for those in need?

   - How does the sharing of our resources demonstrate the love God has for people?

8. **Have someone read 1 Corinthians 16:2 out loud. The Leader summarizes the passage in their own words and lets the group add anything left out. Read the passage a second time, then discuss the questions below.**

   What does this verse tell the church to do?

   - How often are we to do it?

   - How does the verse tell us to decide how much we should set aside, or give?

   - What is the purpose of this collection?

   - When people are hungry or cold, or their homes are flooded, as Christians, how are we to respond?

   - Is God calling you to obey by giving of your resources?

9. **Have someone read Acts 11:27-30 out loud. The Leader summarizes the passage in their own words and lets the group add anything left out. Read the passage a second time, then break into smaller groups to share the story in their own words. Then discuss the questions below.**

   - Who made a prediction?

   - What was the prediction?

   - Did it come to pass?

   - What was the response of the believers?

   - Did everyone give the same amount of money?

» Who was the money collected for?

» How was it sent to the churches who were in need?

» How can we help other churches or individual Christians when they are in need? Should we take offerings regularly?

Leader: Read the following summary to the group.

- The first Christians set aside money each week to give when they met together. The money they gave went to care for the needy among them. At other times they gave to help spread the good news of Jesus. Each person gave according to their ability. Those with more, gave more. Those with less, gave less. Everyone contributed to care for each other. That way everyone's needs were met.

Homework

- The Leader shares the homework with the group and encourages them to complete it before the next meeting.

- **Homework:** Ask the Holy Spirit to speak to your heart about helping a brother or sister in Christ who has needs. What is God challenging you to do? Share that with someone else in your group during the week, and ask them to encourage you to obey the Lord. Share in next week's meeting with the person who you asked to encourage you and tell them how it went.

10. **Collect an Offering**

11. **Share the Lord's Supper**

12. **Closing Prayer**

Chapter 11

Leadership Best Practice #5: Empower God's Saints for Works of Service

Introduction

Jesus movements expand because God's people totally own the mission of God and live out the instructions of Jesus in their everyday lives. Everyone expects to see God work through them, and there is no artificial separation between "clergy" and "laity." This is illustrated by the testimony of Abdul, a factory worker with limited ability to read.

Abdul believed in Christ and was baptized after his neighbor prayed for his sick daughter and she was healed. Abdul had grown up a faithful Muslim and followed the teachings of a renowned Imam. When he was introduced to Christ and became his disciple, Abdul was immediately encouraged to share his experience, in the same way that he had learned about Jesus's love, with his friends and family. Within the first six weeks of his conversion he had baptized five individuals and started a house church, comprised of his family and his neighbor's family.

Over the last four years, Abdul has developed two 5-5-5 networks, which means that he has influenced directly or indirectly over three hundred people toward faith in Jesus Christ. Of course, Abdul did not achieve these accomplishments on his own, as a result of his zeal and passion for God. Nazir, another 5-5-5 leader, has invested in his life. Abdul attended Nazir's LC at least once a month. Even more, Nazir trained Abdul by taking him with him to share Jesus with others, to pray for the sick, and to serve those in need. Nazir told him stories about Jesus, and they discussed together what it meant to obey Christ in the daily situations of life. The fruit of Abdul's life is an overflow of Nazir's empowering. Just like Barnabas was to Paul, so Nazir has been to Abdul.

Jesus movements are full of people like Nazir, who empower others through mentoring, friendship, and walking beside their disciples—releasing them to do the work of the kingdom of God. The Apostle Paul wrote about this kind of empowerment:

> So Christ himself gave the apostles, the prophets, the evangelists, the pastors and teachers, to equip his people for works of service, so that the body of Christ may be built up until we all reach unity in the faith and in the knowledge of the Son of God and become mature, attaining to the whole measure of the fullness of Christ. —Ephesians 4:11–13

> This is not the work of a few or of those who have special skills. Movements arise when everyone gets involved, not just a few.

People are born again into an atmosphere of empowerment because disciple-making is woven into the basic DNA of their lives. When you make a commitment to be a disciple of Jesus Christ in a culture that does not support you, you are entering into a serious, life-changing process. In fact, in most cases where movements are multiplying, becoming a disciple of Jesus requires fundamental life changes. Discipleship, and making new disciples, therefore, is the definition of what it means to follow Christ.

This means that God's leaders are set in the church to equip and empower all of God's people for the works of service that Abdul has been doing. This is not the work of a few or of those who have special skills. Movements arise when everyone gets involved, not just a few.

Leaders Who Empower

Paul's words regarding the gifts of apostles, prophets, evangelists, pastors, and teachers have been a focus of many who write about church leadership. In some cases, this passage is interpreted as prescribing a way of organizing a structure of church leaders that stands in contrast to traditional ways of leading the church. In reality, though, this passage only describes how leadership in the churches operated at the time. I don't think Paul was prescribing a church leadership structure as much as he was simply stating that believers were serving the body of Christ in these capacities.

This is an important distinction. In the book of Acts, we read an account of the movement of the Holy Spirit through the church and how God chose leaders who were tasked with keeping up with what the Spirit was doing. We don't find a detailed guide of how to develop a "biblical" leadership structure. We instead read about leaders who were continuously empowering and equipping people to be disciples of Jesus. Paul was not telling the church at Ephesus to organize in some specific way. He was simply making an observation about the reality of their experience. Christ gave different kinds of leaders to the church to equip people for works of service.

Our experience in movement life confirms this interpretation. In any church system, our human weaknesses mean we can get caught up in titles, positions, job descriptions, and church politics. We may even look for structures that will automatically unlock the magic of the Spirit's movement. This longing to "do it right" often blurs the "right things to do," which may feed the historical distinction between the clergy and the laity.

It seems best simply to concentrate on fostering an environment where all leaders are equipping others, and everyone is concerned with obedience-based discipleship. This is not about titles and designations. It is about how God has raised up leaders in the church. Markus Barth writes about this in his renowned commentary on Ephesians: "The dignity and usefulness of the special ministries given to the church are as great or as small as their effectiveness in making every church member, including the smallest and most despised, an evangelist in his own home and environment."[1]

The word *people* in this passage is better translated as "saints" or "holy ones." God's leaders are set in the church to equip all of God's saints. This destroys any wall that we might assume between clergy and laity. All the people are God's holy ones, set apart for his special service.

Those whom Christ gave as his leaders work alongside all others, not lording over or controlling, but equipping by serving. In this way, the "body of Christ is built up." The Greek word for "built up" here means something like strengthened, edified, or empowered. The role of leaders then is not to perform all the works of service, but to empower others to do works of service so that the churches might "reach unity in the faith."

> Even the leaders who oversee hundreds of thousands of people that meet in house churches are being discipled.

This is an ongoing work of disciple-making through continual training. No one graduates from the school of discipleship. Even the leaders who oversee hundreds of thousands of people that meet in house churches are being discipled. We are living in a system of disciple-makers who are continually being empowered. Let me be concrete. For the past ten years, I have been working with leaders who are caring for hundreds of thousands of disciple-makers. We all meet weekly for ongoing equipping, humbling ourselves before each other. We are all being discipled.

---

1 Barth, *Ephesians 4–6*, 478–80.

We are experiencing the reality of Christ giving leaders who are apostles, prophets, evangelists, pastors, and teachers, although not because we have placed people in these positions. We are not trying to identify who has which of these five gifts so that we can put them in a category or give them a title. We are simply experiencing the work of the Spirit through different kinds of leaders who invest in God's "holy ones." It's not a model to follow. It's a way of life given by the Spirit to obey and enjoy.

The Impediment to Empowerment

James and John were two of the three—Peter was the third—that formed the inner circles of Jesus's twelve disciples. They were invited to experience things with Jesus from which the other nine were excluded. In Mark 10, we read how James and John pulled Jesus aside and said, "Grant us to sit, one at your right hand and one at your left, in your glory" (Mark 10:37 ESV). After two thousand years of church history, we could easily miss the point by assuming that they were asking to be next to Jesus when they arrived in heaven. Or we might think that this is about the return of Jesus at the end time.

Even with good intentions, we may seek to attain influence in the eyes of man and rulership over others.

In the context of first-century Judaism, the "glory" of a potential Messiah referred to the setting up of his administrative rule over Jerusalem. James and John expected Jesus to establish God's kingdom like David and Solomon had once done; and they, as key followers, wanted to be granted special positions of power when Jesus's messianic administration was established.

The transparency of James and John reveals a danger that lies within every heart: that is, the pursuit of power and position. Even with good intentions, we may seek to attain influence in the eyes of man and rulership over others. The church can be seen as a great organization. From "Good to Great" might seduce us to take our eyes off of the role of leaders being servants instead of being served. When the church becomes paramount, instead of being the humble wife of the suffering servant, Jesus Christ, it's easy to slide into seeing ourselves and our roles as people with authority over others, instead of chief servants of all.

Leaders of movements can fall into self-aggrandizement, promoting their work to others, looking for name recognition, while the real work is being done by the Spirit. When God's leaders do this, the attention turns to telling others about how they have succeeded instead of continuing to focus on the power and work of the Holy Spirit through practicing his teachings and the ways of God that have brought success. When the focus is on us, we lose the ability to empower others. If our systems are set up to be easily co-opted by human nature, then we are in trouble. However, if we can translate values like servanthood into practical infrastructure, then we may reduce the place of pride and self-serving taking over. Easily we forget Paul's exhortations that each man's work will be tested and proven by fire in the day of judgment (1 Cor 3:13) and that "the Lord will reward each one for whatever good they do" (Eph 3:8).

A Pathway to Empowering God's Saints

In contrast to the ambition of James and John, which happened during Jesus's ministry and thus before they received the baptism in the Holy Spirit, the leaders of the early churches did not focus on themselves and their own ranks in God's kingdom. They focused, rather, on equipping God's saints for works of service.

Today this empowering and equipping often gets applied to the pulpit ministry of church leaders. However, the early church did not practice a pulpit ministry as we know it in the traditional church, nor do we in movements. Instead, we must search for other ways of applying this passage. We have identified a few key elements to empowerment. They include trust, trustworthiness, communication, and mentoring. The balance of this chapter explores each of these.

Trust

Doing the work of empowering God's people requires that we trust God to work through his people. Our extensive statistical research demonstrated that movements advance when new converts are empowered to baptize those they lead to Christ, as we demonstrated in chapter 6. This means that when only "ordained" leaders are permitted to perform baptisms, lead house-church meetings, and share the sacrament of Christ's body and blood, movements have a difficult time gaining traction.

A disciple-maker told an Imam who had thirty years of experience and hundreds of disciples under his leadership about Jesus, and the Muslim leader committed his life to Christ. One of the Imam's disciples also committed his life to Christ, but he was the first to get baptized. This newly baptized convert then baptized his Imam. Was this baptism ceremony performed to the level that we have grown to expect in the established church? Of course not. It was simple and rudimentary. The disciple-maker who initiated conversations with these men had to release his control of them and trust that they could do it. The key idea to the success of this practice is that the convert repeated what had been done to him. He baptized the way that he himself was baptized.

This principle of trusting others with baptism applies to leading house-church gatherings, sharing one's faith with others, and celebrating the Lord's Supper. All of our people are mentored and learn what to do and how to lead by following the example of those who have brought them to Christ. No one is left alone to figure out how to lead others. First, they experience being led.

> All of our people are mentored and learn what to do and how to lead by following the example of those who have brought them to Christ.

We don't expect them to arrive at some level of perfection before they are released to lead in these ways. They may make some mistakes along the way, of course, but they are supported by the body, and their mentors and those further along in the faith can correct and encourage them. Even more than trusting the people, we are trusting the Holy Spirit who lives within them. They are "holy ones" because the Holy Spirit has taken up residence within their spirit.

Being Trustworthy

Empowerment in a movement is far more than following a list of rules. It is about being the kind of leader that you want others to be. There are many steps in the process of becoming a disciple of Jesus. A transformed life doesn't happen just by learning intellectual knowledge about Jesus, but rather by doing what he says and learning to hear and obey his voice. Paul was clear when he said, "Follow my example, as I follow the example of Christ" (1 Cor 11:1). As our people are transformed by Christ, he empowers them to do his work, his way.

Communication

In chapter 8, I mentioned the book *Turn the Ship Around*, by David Marquet. He was a US Navy captain who was given charge of one of the poorest-performing nuclear submarines in the fleet at the time. When he assumed leadership of this vessel, the sailors operated according to a "Because you told me to" mindset even when they were given commands that they knew were impossible to follow. They were simply workers who followed orders and took no ownership of their work. The previous captain had run a crew who focused on avoiding errors and working harder, even if they were working harder at doing the wrong things. At least they were following the chain of command.

Captain Marquet tells the story of how he led this submarine from worst to first in the fleet through a series of leadership initiatives that empowered the crew to own their work and collaborate as a team. A few of these initiatives directly correlate with what we have experienced in leading a Jesus movement.

First, Marquet writes of shifting from using the language of asking permission to the language of empowerment. When people speak in terms of asking permission, they are buying into a subordinate or passive mindset. They do so when they use phrases like:

- Request permission to …
- I would like to …
- What should I do about …
- What do you think we should …
- Could we …

The language of the empowered helps release them into action. The following might be used by such people:

- I intend to …
- I plan on …
- I will …
- We will …[2]

We see this in the development of our 5-5-5 networks. People are not waiting for a leader above them to tell them exactly what to do. Their passion for Christ and the love that they have received causes them to give that love away in creative ways. While leading a training with hundreds of people who had developed 5-5-5 networks, I was sitting next to a young man who told me how he had started four networks over the last two years. Then he explained his plans for developing his next network. I could not have been prouder of his passion and his total ownership of the goals and process of disciple-making.

 People are not waiting for a leader above them to tell them exactly what to do.

Stephen Covey expands on this in his book *The 8th Habit*, offering simple questions that leaders can use to help God's holy ones make this shift to an empowered mindset. The first question is "How's it going?" In most cases, the leader already knows how things are going. They can see the struggles that house churches are facing, the persecution that is arising, and how people are sharing their faith. It is obvious when 5-5-5 networks are being birthed and when they are not. This question is designed to get on the inside of what is going on, to see what the other person sees that the leader cannot see. It is also designed to explore how God is moving in surprising ways.

---

2 Marquet, *Turn the Ship Around*, 82–83.

Covey's other four empowerment questions derive from the first. They include:

- What are you learning?
- What are your goals?
- How can I help you?
- How am I doing as a helper?[3]

These serve as concrete ways to stimulate conversations that shows care for the person while also supporting them in their movement work.

In addition to fostering empowerment language, Captain Marquet changed the way that leaders talked about solutions. In fact, he resisted the urge to provide answers and strategies, but instead invited them to come up with their own solutions to the challenges that they were facing. In practical terms, he used the following grid as a guideline:

- If the decision needs to be made urgently, make it, then have the team evaluate it.
- If the decision needs to be made reasonably soon, ask for team input, even briefly, then make the decision.
- If the decision can be delayed, then force the team to provide input. Do not force the team to come to consensus; that results in whitewashing differences and dissenting votes. Cherish the dissention. If everyone thinks like you, you don't need them.[4]

This is regularly experienced in our Learning Communities. When we face challenges, the entire team just works together to discover how to move forward. The leader cannot do it alone.

A third way of generating empowering communications occurred as Captain Marquet continually and consistently repeated the message. He states,

Repeat the same message day after day, meeting after meeting, event after event. Sounds redundant, repetitive, and boring. But what's the alternative? Changing the message? That results in confusion and lack of direction.[5]

This is crucial to empowering God's saints because they need clarity about where we are going. In our case, the 5-5-5 strategy is the focus, and it starts immediately after someone is baptized. We want them to know what we are doing and how to get involved right "out of the gate." And then, in every Learning Community, we talk about how we are developing and supporting

---

3 Covey, *8th Habit*, 260–61.

4 Marquet, *Turn the Ship Around*, 151.

5 Marquet, 150.

5-5-5 networks and how house churches are multiplying into other house churches. The language that we use drives our actions, and the actions that we take reinforce that language.

Empowering as a Mentor

When I read the ways that Jesus interacted with the disciples and I observe what is transpiring in our movement, I find that there is a repeated pattern of empowering through mentoring that occurs in seven basic steps. These are:

- Modeling
- Clarification
- Invitation
- Confrontation
- Sending
- Debriefing
- Continuing the Journey

Let's walk through each of these further.

Modeling. Jesus descended from heaven and modeled for us a way of life, as Paul wrote to the Philippians. Jesus did not merely tell us how to live; he showed us. And we are challenged to have the same mind as Christ, "considering others as more important than ourselves" (Phil 2:3 CSB, HCSB, TLV), just as Christ did. He modeled a way of life, a way of ministry that we are to follow; and each of us as leaders should do the same. We are to pray, to share the gospel, to live in humility and servitude, because that is the way of Jesus. I am humbled as I work with leaders who have developed multiple 5-5-5 networks and yet continue to serve with humility. They are modern examples of Paul's statement about modeling.

Paul's statement in Philippians 3:12–17 clearly describes our appropriate role and passion:

> Not that I have already obtained all this, or have already arrived at my goal, but I press on to take hold of that for which Christ Jesus took hold of me. Brothers and sisters, I do not consider myself yet to have taken hold of it. But one thing I do: Forgetting what is behind and straining toward what is ahead, I press on toward the goal to win the prize for which God has called me heavenward in Christ Jesus.
>
> All of us, then, who are mature should take such a view of things. And if on some point you think differently, that too God will make clear to you. Only let us live up to what we have already attained.
>
> Join together in following my example, brothers and sisters, and just as you have us as a model, keep your eyes on those who live as we do.

> Jesus answered the "Why?" question, which is so crucial to empowerment.

Clarification. Jesus did not just model a way of life; he explained why he lived as he did. He taught that his ways were the ways of God, and that if others wanted the blessings of God they would need to repent and participate in God's ways. Jesus answered the "Why?" question, which is so crucial to empowerment. If we fail to explain why we are doing what we are doing, then people will not understand why it is so crucial. They will simply be following a set of rules. We want people to know Jesus and to be able to share their experience with Jesus in a way that is meaningful to them.

Invitation. Empowering God's saints entails an invitation to get involved. Saints are not spectators in the work of other saints. They are all owners of the mission. As I have said many times, we build this into our movement life from day one. No one is left out of getting to join in what God has for them.

Confrontation. The stories of Jesus demonstrate how much energy he spent in challenging the common assumptions that the disciples had about the way God works in the world. Jesus said, "Whoever wants to be my disciple must deny themselves and take up their cross daily and follow me" (Luke 9:23). This is why obedience is crucial to our process. We build the challenge to obey in every part of our life as a movement.

We also ask, "What is God calling us to do in response to this?" This is not something that we do when we see a problem or when someone commits a sin. We assume that we are going to challenge each other to obey in every part of our life together. As we read the Word of God together, we are constantly calling each other to obedience. It is the Word of God—that living, breathing, sharp, and active Word—that confronts, challenges, and in the process, empowers us to do his will, his way.

Sending. In Luke 10, on the heels of clarifying the nature of discipleship at the end of Luke 9, Jesus sent out the 72. This may seem backwards to many because they were not fully developed disciples. We can see that in the rest of Luke's story. Those closest to Jesus failed him on the way to the cross. Yet Jesus sent out the 72 followers in pairs. Jesus knew that the best classroom for educating his followers occurs when they are at work in the field of life.

Movements are catalyzed by young followers who realize that they are sent. Responding to the call of Christ from their earliest point of conversion sets their passion for discipleship ablaze. It opens their hearts and minds to the need to learn more. They are sent with the little that they know and as they obey, the transformative power in the seed is released and they are changed, transformed. Jesus gave his disciples the Word day by day. As they obeyed, the power that is in the seed of the Word was released in their hearts. This is the pattern of discipleship that Jesus practiced. It was more than intellectual understanding of truth. He was the truth, the Word made flesh. As his disciples received by faith his Word and obeyed it, they were being changed into his likeness.

> Debriefing is crucial to obedience, because all of us can fall into the trap of saying the right things when we're together, while failing to act when we're apart.

Debriefing. After Jesus sent out the 72, they returned for a time of dialogue with Jesus where they reported what they saw and learned through the experience. They had much to learn, even though they had seen some immediate success. Their eternal status was much more crucial than the short-term impact of ruling over the demonic. Jesus helped them see how to evaluate what was truly meaningful.

The same is true of movement life. On the surface, one might assume that house churches operate in isolation from each other, and in some cases this is true. But in movements that have sustaining power over the long haul, continual interactive empowerment occurs.

This is one reason we developed Learning Communities, so that we could debrief regularly as we are working to obey Christ in our context. Debriefing is crucial to obedience, because all of us can fall into the trap of saying the right things when we're together, while failing to act when we're apart.

Continuing the Journey. I stated this earlier, but it bears repeating—no one outgrows the need for empowerment. It is continual because it occurs along the path of following Jesus, not as an up-front transfer of information. We currently have eight leaders who each oversee tens of thousands of people meeting in house churches as they work together to lead this movement. None of them have graduated to a level of maturity in which they don't need ongoing empowerment. They need God's Spirit to flow into them for the work that they are doing today: a fresh encounter of God's gifts flowing through each other and new insights that will equip them for new challenges. These men regularly dig into God's Word together, learning how to study it together and encourage and strengthen each other from it.

Conclusion

Kasem accepted the Lord as his personal Savior, and his house-church leader taught him about putting his faith into action and sharing his faith by leading five others to Christ. However, he didn't have time to do so because he was moving to another country. Even after moving, he remained connected to his leader, who mentored him over the phone and encouraged him to start his own 5-5-5 network.

Meanwhile, after working in a foreign country as a housekeeper for a year, Tawfiq, a fellow worker in the home, got sick and Kasem went to his house to pray for his healing. After Tawfiq was miraculously healed, the two grew close and Tawfiq showed interest in Jesus.

Kasem told Tawfiq stories from the Bible and eventually led him to the Lord. Then Kasem began mentoring Tawfiq, and they went together to find 5 of Tawfiq's friends and family members whom they could disciple. Tawfiq baptized 5 of them within two months. Kasem met regularly with them and encouraged them to go and find 5 others to disciple. In three months, they had all reached their 5 each with the gospel, totaling 25, and then these 25 reached 155 new believers, who were baptized, within a year. This occurred because of life-on-life mentoring, which is the basis of obedience-based discipleship. Kasem and Tawfiq learned to follow Jesus as they obeyed, and they lived out their faith by giving it away to others. All these new believers were empowered from the day of their baptism to share the Gospel and reach their friends and families with the love of Jesus Christ.

The need for empowerment never ceases. However, there are many impediments, such as human ambition and pride, authoritarian attitudes, wanting to be served, a love of position and others. Mentoring, taking a servant's attitude, loving with humble attitude while looking for ways to serve both the person and the Word of God are some of the ways of empowering others.

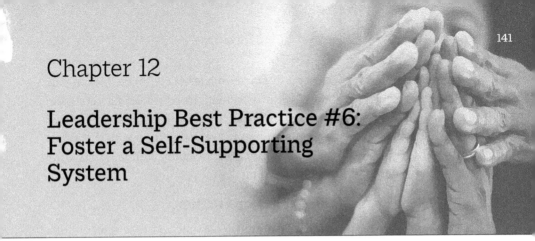

Chapter 12

Leadership Best Practice #6: Foster a Self-Supporting System

Introduction

Henry Venn was a nineteenth-century missionary leader who developed what is known as the "three-self formula." In response to his observations about missionary work during his time, he concluded that most missionaries were far too dependent upon resources from the West. National Christians in Africa, Asia, and South America were led to Christ and participated in churches in ways that created a perpetual dependence upon resources from Western churches. He challenged this pattern by promoting the goal of fostering churches that are self-governing, self-propagating, and self-supporting. The goal was to develop indigenous churches that are not dependent upon the leadership of missionaries, missionary organizations, or funds that flow in from outside the local context.

Venn argued that this would result in what he called "the euthanasia of a mission," where missionary organizations would become unnecessary and missionaries would work themselves out of their jobs. He wrote,

> Regarding the ultimate object of a mission, viewed under its ecclesiastical aspect, to be the settlement of a native Church, under native pastors, upon a self-supporting system, it should be borne in mind that the progress of a mission mainly depends upon the training up and the location of native pastors; and that, as it has been happily expressed, "the euthanasia of a mission" takes place when a missionary, surrounded by well-trained native congregations, under native pastors, is able to resign all pastoral work into their hands.[1]

The end goal of movement work should never be the advancement of the missionary organization or the missionary. We are not raising money so that

---

1 Knight, *Missionary Secretariat of the Rev. Henry Venn*, 307; quoted in Shenk, "Contribution of Henry Venn to Mission Thought," 25–42.

people can become dependent upon funds from other countries. Movements flourish when they heed the three-self formula in which leaders are from the local context and growth occurs through the work of those within that context. In addition, we design the organization so that the goal is that funds for the budget can be raised from within the movement churches so that we are not dependent upon external funding.

Taking It a Step Further

Henry Venn's teachings were radical during his day, and they remain quite radical today. This is especially true of the principle of self-supporting. The life of Jesus movements being able to sustain their networks in the decades ahead partly depends upon leaders embracing this mindset. When I began my work in Southeast Asia, I didn't want to develop any strategy that depended upon me being personally present or, in the long term, upon financial resources from Western organizations. In fact, we have resisted any strategies that required external funding, even when organizations wanted to give us money. We knew that if we wanted to see a movement that grew in an organic and self-sustaining way, it must be largely self-supporting from the start.

> We knew that if we wanted to see a movement that grew in an organic and self-sustaining way, it must be largely self-supporting from the start.

I entered this work with no ambition to develop a missionary organization that funneled funds from the West to developing nations. In fact, many who have supported me financially have inquired about why we have set up things as we have. They want to know why we don't have a larger organization, more trainers, more fundraising, and more money flowing through our systems to the "mission field."

Many organizations that are doing movement work take a different approach than we have taken. They raise money and use funds to attain a hearing for the gospel in a local context through various projects, such as schools, orphanages, medical facilities, etc. This money opens doors for the gospel in the minds and hearts of those whom they impact, and then the purpose of the foreign money is served.

In my personal experience, however, this approach sets the stage for financial dependency by the "have nots" upon the "haves" that can be very difficult to change later. I think some of the best commonsense wisdom about this is, "The way you start is the way you finish." When people hear the gospel introduced using money, then Western wealth will always be associated with the kingdom of God. In many cases, this results in more harm than good. Missionary theologian Miriam Adeney illustrates this with a story she heard from an African Christian.

> Elephant and Mouse were best friends. One day Elephant said, "Mouse, let's have a party!" Animals gathered from far and near. They ate. They drank. They sang. And they danced. And nobody celebrated more and danced harder than Elephant. After the party was over, Elephant exclaimed, "Mouse, did you ever go to a better party? What a blast!" But Mouse did not answer.
>
> "Mouse, where are you?" Elephant called. He looked around for his friend, and then shrank back in horror. There at Elephant's feet lay Mouse. His little body was ground into the dirt. He had been smashed by the big feet of his exuberant friend, Elephant. "Sometimes, that is what it is like to do mission with you Americans," the African storyteller commented. "It is like dancing with an Elephant."[2]

We have good intentions. We aim to be generous and help those in need, but our efforts actually undermine the development of a movement. And like the elephant, we don't even see what we are doing. We develop a system that sets up the outsider in a position of power so that those in developing nations depend upon those who control the money.

In their book *When Helping Hurts*, Steven Corbett and Brian Fikkert define these issues with startling words. They propose that the rich are trying to "save" the poor, rather than trusting God to do the work of salvation within the means of the local context. They even go so far as to say that those giving the money can develop a "god-complex."

> One of the biggest problems in many poverty-alleviation efforts is that their design and implementation exacerbates the poverty of being of the economically rich—their god-complexes—and the poverty of being of the economically poor—their feelings of inferiority and shame. The way that we act toward the economically poor often communicates—albeit unintentionally—that we are superior and they are inferior. In the process we hurt the poor and ourselves. And here is the clincher: this dynamic is likely to be particularly strong whenever middle-to-upper-class, North American Christians try to help the poor, given these Christians' tendency toward a Western, materialistic perspective of the nature of poverty.[3]

Do those of us with money tend to develop such a god-complex? I am not able to answer this question as I'm not the judge of others' hearts, but this scenario represents a potential trap for well-intended Christians who want to help.

---

2 Adeney, *Daughters of Islam*, 189.

3 Corbett and Fikkert, *When Helping Hurts*, 62.

For several decades I have had the privilege of taking hundreds of my fellow American believers to do missionary work around the world. It seems to me that believers with a heart for missions, including those who don't travel overseas but stay at home and support missions, tend to think that money is the answer to every problem. As the saying goes, "When the only tool you have is a hammer, every problem looks like a nail." It is heartbreaking for Americans to visit places like Haiti and other developing nations. When seeing such poverty, we tend to view our bank accounts as the only tool in the tool chest. However, money can be a source of great destruction as well as great blessing.

Quality research has been done on this phenomenon, called "The Law of the Instrument," which affects all aspects of life. In 1981, psychology professor Thomas Gilovich conducted a study at Stanford University with International Conflict students. Here's a quote from this study:

> The *Law of the Instrument* is about cognitive bias. It's about relying on your existing memory-bank of approaches, tools or analogies to solve *every* problem. But the Thomas Gilovich experiment goes further still; it suggests that you can have a rich and varied box of tools, but if the problem bears even the tiniest resemblance to a nail, then out comes the hammer. And the person wielding the hammer won't even realize it.[4]

At some point when we were visiting orphanages in Russia, prisons in Peru, and dozens of other desperately challenging environments, I would ask my fellow Americans to check in with me if they wanted to give cash to those we encountered. Out of a good heart, we so want to help, and we just don't realize that money can do harm rather than help. This is even more true when we have a long-term goal of establishing reproducing, disciple-making communities in nations and people groups where the gospel has not been preached. In fact, it is more critical that we don't view poverty as a nail and bring out our hammer if we want to establish faith communities that are self-sustaining and capable of reaching their own people with the love of Jesus Christ.

In the 5-5-5 model, we begin with self-propagation. Those whose lives have been impacted by faith in Jesus through hearing the Word carry this Good News to friends and family, sometimes accompanied by healings, dreams, miracles, or simply the testimony of a family member or friend. The spreading of a Jesus movement depends upon those within the movement, not leaders from the outside, from the very beginning.

---

4 Gilovich, "Seeing the Past in the Future," 801.

Those who develop 5-5-5 networks and start additional networks naturally "govern" because they are the leaders who mentored other leaders. Now we are touching on self-governance as well as being self funding.

> No one is paid a salary, and there is little to no financial support infused in the system from the West.

We are self-supporting because we teach everyone to give money to the Lord from the very beginning. They are taught biblically and shown how to give instead of being given to. No one is paid a salary, and there is little to no financial support infused in the system from the West.

This means that we take Venn's three-self formula a step further. Rather than having it as a goal for the future of mission work, we have learned to start movements with the three-self mindset from the very beginning. Again, "The way you start is the way you will finish" has served as a guiding principle for us, and it continues to bear fruit. This means that we don't start with money from developed nations and then wean the movement off of that money at a certain point. We begin the movement assuming that we have no money from external sources.

The Barrier of Institutional Paradigms

Many people who hear me talk about money in this way assume that such an approach is not actually possible. Usually, our conversation reveals that the issue is not a spiritual issue related to a lack of faith, or something of that kind. Rather, most of us have a paradigm problem. The mental picture that defines how missionary work should be accomplished doesn't allow us to think creatively enough to imagine how self-supporting can actually work. There are two specific issues that hinder us.

The first mental image that hinders us is the way we think a church should function. Typically, this means that a church is truly a church when it has a brick-and-mortar building, or at least a stick hut with a roof, and also established leadership. The second blocking paradigm can be the missionary organization, even those that have the goal of fostering a Jesus movement. Most organizations typically have layers of leadership, governing boards, fundraising strategies, and, of course, missionaries who are sent out to do the work of starting and sustaining movements. Some of these organizations are tied to denominations, some to specific churches, and some operate independently.

Both churches and missionary organizations can play important roles in what God is doing in developing Jesus movements. Regarding the church, if you have made it this far in the book, it should be obvious that house churches in a Jesus movement operate differently from the common ways that we have assumed church structures should operate. However, the church itself is crucial to movement life.

> If our time and resources focus on creating a sustainable US-based missionary organization, then our very existence can become a barrier to our missionary efforts.

In addition, there are many fruitful ministries and missionary organizations that have played a central role in fostering movements. In fact, the work that I do is done through a small non-profit ministry that has the sole aim of fostering Jesus movements. However, if our time and resources focus on creating a sustainable US-based missionary organization, then our very existence can become a barrier to our missionary efforts. This seems like a catch-22 position to be in. Do I focus my time and work on raising money so that I can initiate and cultivate movements overseas, or do I focus my time and energy on doing the work of movement development and trust God for the money to support myself and my family?

I have chosen the latter, and so far God has been faithful to provide the funds. I'm not trying to build an organization in the US that will outlive me. If someone is going to carry on this work beyond me, the Holy Spirit will have to show them how to live and do this good work. Probably that will be leaders in the movements I have started who find ways to continue the work.

Roland Allen elaborates on this topic, saying:

> There is a horrible tendency for an organization to grow in importance till it overshadows the end of its existence, and begins to exist for itself. … The maintenance of the organization has become a greater incentive to work than the purpose for which it was first created.[5]

Another common problem is the insistence on replicating doctrines and practices of a particular denomination. I have been in churches around the world whose worship and practices are the same as the parent denomination in the US. Regardless of being in Moscow, New Delhi, or Buenos Aires, if we could just change the language to English, then we would be singing the same songs, preaching similar sermons, and being as comfortable as if we were at our local church at home. This is the ultimate goal of many mission organizations, and it creates a barrier to reaching the goal of the three-self approach.

If we are to use local music to sing Scripture songs so that we touch the hearts of the people, give the house churches freedom to organize their meetings, and minister as the Lord leads them. Then the gatherings will be

---

5 Allen, *Spontaneous Expansion*, 98.

quite different from our local church meetings—not just smaller, but more like small-group meetings. I have been in many meetings where the music was very foreign to me personally, but the believers were really energized by it and learned much Scripture from the songs.

The two issues of focusing on the church as an institution and the mission entity as an organization will obviously directly influence how we use money. The official vision might focus on making disciples who make disciples, but the day-to-day energy of the organization revolves around running the organization for the sake of keeping the organizational doors open and people employed. It assumes that God's work depends upon the development of elaborate organizations. Allen writes, "Our love of organization leads us to rely on it."[6]

Organizational focus requires us to focus on money, because maintaining the existence of an organization—even if it fails to meet its stated goals—depends upon funding. In fact, we often get caught in the money trap. If we are successful at raising money and throwing it at mission efforts, then we think that we must be successful. Success is measured in dollars, and the lack of money handicaps our work and stalls the vision. If this had been the paradigm in New Testament days, I doubt if the church would even exist today.

> The size of the organization determines the effectiveness of the work, in this way of thinking. It couldn't be more wrong.

This kind of thinking can dominate mission work. We begin a work, raise funds, recruit teams, write reports, and promote our work so that we can raise more funds, recruit more teams, write more reports, and promote our work more. All the while, we assume that if we are doing more with a larger organization, then we must be accomplishing the purpose for which we exist. The size of the organization determines the effectiveness of the work, in this way of thinking. It couldn't be more wrong.

This is the way that institutionalization values and practices subvert original intentions. Many of our great Western universities are an example of this phenomenon. They began with clear purpose where the Bible was taught, but now they are so focused on staying in business that they are steeped in unbelief and even anti-Christian teachings. We start doing the work for the sake of the vision, but then we shift to doing the work to maintain the organization, believing that our existence must signify success.

In the development of elaborate organizations, we are working against movement growth because we are asking the organization to produce something that does not align with it. Allen continues:

6 Allen, 99.

Not only does our love of organization lead us to expect from it spiritual results, it also leads us to ascribe to it results which do not belong to it. … [We have] a tendency to believe that the great success of our modern missionary work is due to our splendid organization, while all history shows that success as great, and, perhaps, of a deeper character, has been attained without any such organization as ours.[7]

> The key to a flourishing Jesus movement is to do the work of a movement—to make disciple-makers who continuously multiply more disciple-makers and organically develop churches of the new disciples in which they nourish each other in the Word of God.

We want the spiritual results of movement growth, but we end up investing our time in running the organization. Think of it this way: we read the book of Acts and see the dynamic life of the early church. We set a goal to do what they did: to pray, to share the faith, to make disciples, to gather in simple, relational ways. We see fruit from this, and then we begin to develop an organization to support the maintenance of that fruit. This organization requires money to pay those who run the organization, to plan meetings, and to manage the flow of money. What began as a simple system becomes one that has multiple layers of complexity, and to keep that complexity in check we must add multiple layers of administration for the sake of accountability.

In addition, we have not even talked about how we must build brick-and-mortar offices and gathering venues to make this organization work. The organizational mindset is so common that we don't even question it. Roland Allen's statement above simply points out that we cannot expect this organizational mindset to produce the spiritual results that we find in the book of Acts. It's akin to expecting a football team to win football games because they are simply members of a team. The key to being effective at playing football is to play the game of football well. We must block and tackle and do the things that will win a game.

Recently a major US denomination sold a huge office building in my city for tens of millions of dollars. I wonder if their real-estate department is connecting to their vision of making disciples. A better question is why they allowed the organization to become so complex and how the players saw their roles contributing to making disciples.

The key to a flourishing Jesus movement is to do the work of a movement—to make disciple-makers who continuously multiply more disciple-makers and organically develop churches of the new disciples in which they nourish

---

7 Allen, 99–100.

each other in the Word of God. A movement can be self-sustaining when we teach them to take care of the needs of each other and those in their communities from the beginning. When Jesus faced the hungry crowd of five thousand and his disciples came to him, he said, "You feed them" (Mark 6:32–44). The resources for the harvest are in the harvest, not in the Western church. That doesn't mean that we cannot carefully invest Western resources to help the fledgling movement, but only with great care.

> People make disciples.
> Organizations don't.
> The churches are simply a
> fruit of disciple-making.

Jesus didn't start or invest in an organization. He didn't command his disciples to go out and start churches. Rather, he told them to make disciples: "Teaching them all that I have commanded you" (Matt 28:20). He really said that we should make disciples who make disciples, or make disciple-makers. He didn't challenge his followers to develop institutions. For generations we have taught the Great Commission, and our organizational mindset has caused us to miss this point. We tend to conclude that he told us to build churches of brick and mortar so that we can make disciples. But he told us to make disciples and teach them to make disciple-makers.

People make disciples. Organizations don't. The churches are simply a fruit of disciple-making. When the church or mission entity begins to exist for itself, then disciple-making will stall. Jesus didn't tell us to "plant churches"—a popular term and paradigm in missionary work today. This changes the focus in a critical way and we can stall out, missing the greatest opportunity for growing mass movements to faith in Christ in the history of Christianity.

All of this is directly related to the use of money. Since most movements that are expanding exponentially are occurring in non-Western contexts, it is assumed that they need Western money to make disciples. But this is only true if we conclude that movements depend upon organizations.

For instance, in a movement context one man went out to a village to share Christ with a relative of his neighbor who lived near him. In six months, the responsive man of peace had led to the development of seven 5-5-5 networks, which means that over a thousand people have been baptized and are now disciple-makers, who meet in about 150 house churches. However, there was no "church planting" organization or other institution that planned for this event. Spontaneous growth is a sign of movements.

This man did not share the gospel to be paid or for other financial reasons. None of the leaders within this network are paid. The only cost is that the missionary receives some personal support from the networks that he has already developed so that he can be freed up to travel and start this new work. This story could be repeated thousands of times because it is a sign of the life of the Holy Spirit in a movement. Without this life, we do not have a living organism, but rather a dull organization trying to achieve supernatural goals with human effort and organization.

This is possible because we have developed a system that operates around relational connections as opposed to institutional development. The missionary is not trying to establish an organization called church. He is making disciples who then can make disciples. All of this is done through the 5-5-5 system.

Systems That Depend upon External Funding

The system that you develop will determine the funding that you will need. Many try to establish movements in ways that require elaborate organizations because they have developed systems that require funding. This usually comes in two forms.

The Access-Ministry System

The first system is called access ministries. With this approach, a missionary organization may develop strategies to gain access to an unreached group to receive permission to share the gospel. These strategies come in the form of things like providing medical care, offering food, training in agricultural methods, clean water, education, disaster relief, etc. After these services provide a benefit to the community, the missionary then will be able to share the gospel.

There is no doubt that these services are needed, there is definitely a place for them in missionary work, and that access ministry can certainly open doors for the gospel. This may be done using local believers who serve without pay to open hearts among the closed communities. However, the challenge comes when we develop a system that makes the success of a movement dependent upon outside funding.

Access ministries most often depend upon fundraising outside of the context of the local community in need. If a movement opens doors in a community with foreign money, that creates a natural dependence on outside funding, and usually it will need to continue this outside funding to continue to suceed. In the West, the idea is sold by showing how more money gains more access for the gospel. However, it's often not mentioned that when individuals come to Christ through an access ministry, they will expect that the way they were introduced to Christ is the way that they will lead others to Christ. "Go and do what has been done to you," is often a mantra that's useful.

This is the normal way that the gospel spreads from one individual to another. Thus, the new convert will have his hand out for money from the West to provide a service to his neighbor that will open the door for the gospel. This paradigm has dependency built in it and therefore cannot spread like wildfire without always increasing Western money. The key fundraiser must work harder in the Western context to find ever more money.

As stated above, instead of a self-supporting system, you end up with a perpetually dependent system. In his classic work, *The Indigenous Church*, published in 1976, Melvin Hodges wrote about the importance of developing a self-supporting system from the onset.

> Laying the right foundation from the very beginning of the work is essential. The procedures established with the first few converts in the first church will become the pattern followed by believers and churches that spring up later.[8]

> If you initiate a system that depends upon outside funding, then the maintenance of that system will depend upon outside funding.

If you initiate a system that depends upon outside funding, then the maintenance of that system will depend upon outside funding. This, of course, will require the development of an institution that will serve as the means for raising and distributing those funds. If funds from the West stop, the whole system collapses.

There are those who understand the pitfalls of using access ministries as described and who plug in a simple servant approach by encouraging individuals or small groups with local funding to help those around them in projects that still open the hearts and minds of people needing to hear the gospel. For example, when a disciple-maker sees a local farm worker in the field, he may voluntarily choose to spend a few hours helping him at no charge. This will typically open the farmer's heart to a new relationship, and to at least hearing the gospel.

The Paid House-Church Leader System

Another common system that is not self-supporting is one where house-church leaders are compensated for their leadership. In a flourishing movement, leadership of house churches arises organically because people are leading people to Christ, baptizing them, and making disciples. It occurs along relational lines, not through formal appointments by those who are in control.

---

8 Hodges, *Indigenous Church*, 82.

This is difficult for many who are rooted in traditional ways of the church to grasp, because paying local converts has been a long-standing pattern of missionary work. We have wed dollars to leadership. If a missionary reports to supervisors back home that he has a growing number of leaders of churches who need financial support, then it is easy to raise money because this is the assumed way that church leadership works. However, this mindset undermines movements for the following reasons:

1. Paying a convert to lead a church ties their discipleship to employment. As a result, instead of obeying because they have received God's love and they love God, they obey so that they can become a leader themselves and get paid. House churches are often led by people who have been converts for less than a year. We must protect them from this temptation.

2. Financial compensation can cause pride and competition between leaders. We want a system that keeps the house-church leaders focused on what God is calling them to do, not on how the gospel can be used to help them become recipients of Western funding.

3. Paying leaders can create a poaching system where house-church leaders align themselves with the highest bidder. Often a missionary leader from a Western organization will tell movement leaders, "It's not right. You should be paid. And we will pay you if you want to be part of our denomination or mission organization."

4. An employment system tends to hinder voluntary work. Movements do not expand because leaders are getting paid to do the work. They expand because new converts are sharing their story with others. They do so because they have received eternal life and the Holy Spirit has empowered them.

5. When people in a local setting learn that Christian leaders are being paid by Western funding, they tend to trust the message less. The gospel is more likely to be viewed as a form of Western propaganda as opposed to the truth about how God is transforming people in a local context.

6. Paying leaders creates dependence upon outside funding. If you pay church leaders for fulfilling the biblical mandate of making disciples, how many hundreds of thousands of them can you pay if you're trying to reach a large population. The money for this kind of staffing is not available within the local economy, where the typical worker may earn a dollar or two per day.[9]

---

9 This list is adapted from the work of John Nevius and applied to a movement context. See Nevius, *Planting and Development of Missionary Churches*.

In our system, we do not need to pay house-church leaders. They simply serve in this capacity because they are making disciples. Not only that, but we also do not pay those who are developing or have developed 5-5-5 networks, which is typically comprised of twenty to twenty-five organically organized house churches. When a person has developed two 5-5-5 networks, they may be sent out as a missionary and receive some support from those within the networks he has developed. We may invest a percentage of support from outside in this case, but the goal and approach is always full indigenous support and whatever outside money is used is always temporary and terminal.

Generosity

What we do with money depends upon the training we provide on the biblical principle of generosity. The Apostle Paul wrote, "Each of you should give what you have decided in your heart to give, not reluctantly or under compulsion, for God loves a cheerful giver" (2 Cor 9:7). The following is a quote from the lesson that we teach in our Learning Communities and pass on to house churches:

> When we trust God to care for us, and when we trust him and give our money and resources to help meet needs, we can give to others out of a cheerful heart. We don't do this because we are forced to give. We can trust that God will replenish our resources both to take care of us and to give to others again. We don't have to give of our money because it is a rule that we must follow. We give generously and joyfully because we get to give. We give because we love God and want to bless others! We recognize that God is the source of all things and that God takes care of us. Our life does not depend upon how much money we have or do not have. Our life depends upon God. It is a joy to be able to bless others.

The goal is to share with those who have a need and to propagate the gospel to areas that have not been exposed to God's love. Paul wrote:

> Our desire is not that others might be relieved while you are hard pressed, but that there might be equality. At the present time your plenty will supply what they need, so that in turn their plenty will supply what you need. The goal is equality, as it is written: "The one who gathered much did not have too much, and the one who gathered little did not have too little."
> —2 Corinthians 8:13–15

The first Christians set aside money each week to give when they met together. The money they gave went to care for the needy among them. At other times they gave to help spread the good news of Jesus. Each person gave according to their ability. Those with more, gave more. Those with less, gave less. Everyone contributed to care for each other. That way everyone's needs were met.

In most movement settings, typically the people are not wealthy. They have never practiced generosity like that taught in the Scriptures. In a house church there may only be one or two wage earners. As they learn to give generously, the people that they are helping with funds are blessed. The point is not how much but training them to trust God so that they are free to give to others who are in need.

A Self-Funding Missionary Strategy

As stated previously, our goal in a Jesus movement is not simply to develop indigenous churches. It is to be indigenous from the very beginning. To explain the difference, it's helpful to compare indigenization with indigeneity. With a strategy of indigenization, missionaries create well-organized churches and then hand them over to local converts. The foreign mission is generally seen as a scaffolding which must be removed once the fellowship of believers is functioning properly. Missionaries first evangelize and then establish the church by doing the work of ministry themselves. They provide teaching, pastoral care, sacraments, buildings, finance, and authority. Eventually they train local converts to take over these responsibilities. Thus, the church becomes indigenous as it becomes self-supporting, self-propagating, and self-governing.

A strategy of indigeneity operates from a different point of view. Missionaries do not create churches but focus on helping local converts develop their own spiritual gifts and leadership abilities and organize their own house churches. Of course, the Scriptures provide the basic paradigm as to the practices and values of the disciples' life together, with an emphasis on reading and obeying the teachings of Jesus. Missionaries, converts to the gospel themselves, are sent out to make disciples and help them make their own disciples from the very beginning. The churches that arise out of this work are thus indigenous from the start. They begin as self-supporting, self-propagating, and self-governing.

In our setting, we send out missionaries, each of which has developed at least two 5-5-5 networks. They are provided with some support from the generosity of the house churches in those networks, and they go into new villages or segments of the population where the gospel has not been established. As mentioned, we may provide a percentage of outside support, but this percentage is reduced annually. This expansion of the gospel is done along relational lines. Those who go into a new neighborhood to share the gospel with a friend or relative of someone in their networks, or if there are no connections, then the worker focuses on finding a person of peace, which could be a man or woman who is open to the Gospel in order to initiate the 5-5-5 network developing process. We are not a church planting organization, but rather a network developing movement.

> The indigenous missionary does not need to remain present to establish organizational systems. He makes disciples and shows his disciples how to do likewise.

This approach is totally dependent upon social networks and using the raw power of signs and wonders and God's Word to penetrate the hearts of unbelievers (Heb 4:12). We pray for and see healings, speak the living Word of God, inspire hope for the freedom from sin, and offer the free gift of eternal life. As a missionary shares the gospel, he is looking for a person of peace (see Luke 10:2–12), someone who is both open to the gospel and has influence upon others in their social network. As I shared earlier, one of our missionaries traveled to a new area and led one person to Christ. He then helped this new Christian share about his encounter with God, and ten others were baptized. Of those, seven have developed their own 5-5-5 networks, representing over one thousand new disciple-makers. Recently forty-two new believers were baptized together when one woman shared with her friends about Jesus dying in their place for their sins.

This simple system spreads the gospel along relational lines, which can be done with limited financial cost from outside, except for a percentage of help for the missionary who was initially sent. The indigenous missionary does not need to remain present to establish organizational systems. He makes disciples and shows his disciples how to do likewise. Once the system is established, he can oversee the work and develop house-church leaders and 5-5-5 leaders through Learning Communities, which are vital to the long-term success of the movement.

Chapter 13

Leadership Best Practice #7: Develop Patterns That Are Reproducible

Introduction

Throughout this book, I have highlighted stories like that of Amal. He was born into a Muslim family but was not overly zealous about his faith. When Amal heard about Isa, he was skeptical at first because of previous exposure to Western missionaries. But he worked every day alongside his friend, Haris, during harvest season. Haris kept telling him about how Isa had given him hope after going through a tough time when his son died.

Eventually Amal gave his life to Christ and was baptized, and Haris invited him to a meeting in his house. He already knew those who attended because they were all from the same community, but Amal was surprised that Haris actually led the meeting since he had only been a disciple of Christ for less than a year. Within six months, Amal had led five others to Christ and was also leading a church in his home.

In most religious settings, people like Amal and Haris would be the exceptions. They would be zealots with infectious, charismatic personalities whose commitments towered over the norms. In a Jesus movement, though, they are not unique. Movement advancement—through disciple-makers making disciple-makers—depends upon average people being released to trust God to work through them in inspiring ways.

Rather than depending upon uniquely gifted individuals doing powerfully spectacular acts, everyone gets involved from the very beginning. And by "everyone," I mean the newest of disciples. These baby believers don't wait until they attain an acceptable level of maturity before they are challenged to serve and obey. They know that being a Christ-follower means actively following, as we discussed in chapter 10 when we laid out the importance of obedience-based discipleship.

One of the reasons why we can tell stories like those of Amal and Haris is the fact that everything we do is highly reproducible. We have worked with great diligence to avoid complication. Our goal is to create a pattern that Amal can follow, Haris can observe and experience, and then Haris is able to imitate what he saw Amal do. The following identifies the key principles of this practice that makes multiplication work in our movements.

The Principle of Simplicity

The degree to which our activities are reproducible is the degree to which a movement can expand. The greater the reproducibility, the greater potential for movement growth. We are focusing on the discipleship practices of life together. The more complex we make a task, such as sharing communion or baptism, the less likely others will be able to repeat the experience, because it requires training or even a credentialed expert to execute the sacraments.

> The more complex we make a task, the less likely others will be able to repeat the experience, because it requires training at best or even a credentialed expert to execute the sacraments.

We have seen this at play in the church for centuries. Since the time of Constantine, when the church was officially sanctioned by the Roman government and the pagan temples were re-purposed for Christian worship, the way that the church operated depended upon the leadership of experts. The clergy had to receive years of formal education to lead a worship service. Only the ordained were permitted to baptize and to serve communion. Within the Catholic Church, this expertise was taken a step even further because it was reserved for the celibate.

Ever since the days of Luther and Calvin, however, Protestant churches have also fostered the value of the religious expert. Because discipleship has been primarily information-based instead of obedience-based, Christian growth has depended on the tutelage of experts who possess comprehensive knowledge to teach "the laity." But the development of such experts limits reproducibility.

First, a person must have the cultural background and capacity to learn information, as well as the opportunity to attend a traditional school. Normally this means leaving their own local church context, and through the process of advanced training, they often lose their cultural identity. They are no longer seen as a contextual insider when they return and may struggle to find the effectiveness that they had experienced before going away to advanced schooling.

This is not to denigrate the importance of theology and biblical interpretation. Throughout this book, I have drawn from advanced resources that have helped me better articulate a biblically-shaped view of movements. However, the leaders in our movements do not need to possess the ability to articulate these biblical perspectives to be used by the Spirit in reaping a mighty harvest.

I am reiterating observations made by Donald McGavran when he was a missionary in India. He saw expert missionaries who had extensive training work for decades with very little fruit as they developed missionary stations. To be a Christ-follower, the local converts had to enter into the life of the missionary station and learn a new culture. Those called to lead had to attend school and become like Western Christians. Everything was complex and not reproducible. How could a grassroots person repeat what they were learning from the foreign missionary unless they became like the foreign missionary?

Of course, missionary stations have long passed as models for missions. However, the missionary-station mindset can continue in our work. We can inadvertently remain unnecessarily complex and fail to see how we are forcing people to adopt Western church patterns that require training to do things that do not naturally fit their context.

We have protected our movements from the concept that leaders must receive intensive outside training to qualify for roles in his body. The principle of simplicity is woven into our thinking.

The Power of Modeling

Obedience-based discipleship is not only rooted in the importance of personal commitments to obedience to Christ, but also in watching others who are obeying. Younger disciple-makers learn how to be effective disciple-makers as they walk alongside those who are more experienced in obeying Christ. The old saying, "Do as I do, not just what I say," applies here. Curtis Sergeant teaches the mother-duck principle. The ducklings follow the lead of the duck in front of them, who follows the mother duck. This way the whole brood can be led as they imitate each other, following the lead of their parent.

Paul wrote to the church in Corinth, "Even if you had ten thousand tutors in Christ, you do not have many fathers, for in Christ Jesus I became your father through the gospel. Therefore, I urge you to imitate me" (1 Cor 4:15–16 NASB). In this passage Paul is confronting the influence of voices who were offering "expert" advice to the church that was complicating the gospel. He referred to them as "tutors," a word that was used of a person who was paid to guide the education of young children. A tutor focused on information, and Paul said that there were many such voices. But there are few "fathers" who are willing to lay down their lives for those that are their spiritual children and who are invested in modeling life for children.

> We might receive teaching from experts, but we will learn how to live—obedience-based formation—from those who invest in us.

We might receive teaching from experts, but we will learn how to live—obedience-based formation—from those who invest in us. This kind of learning is akin to a boy learning how to farm from his father or a daughter learning to care for a home from her mother. We learn about these things through imitation. Paul urged the Corinthians "to imitate me," to copy how he followed Jesus. He was their spiritual parent, one who had given his life for them, at cost to his own well-being.

This kind of impartation can only occur through life-on-life modeling, which is something that anyone can do. The least educated person can show another person what it means to obey. In the case of Haris in the story at the beginning of this chapter, he is not able to read, but he knows how to love people. It is common for him to pray for the needs of others for hours at a time. One of the things that convinced Amal to become a follower of Jesus was the miraculous recovery of his mother after Haris prayed for her.

The Principle of Focusing on the End User

Movements advance at the edges, at the point of new disciple-makers sharing their faith with friends and family members. They don't grow by drawing people to the center but as the edges roll out into new spaces. This means that the "end user," to use a modern commercial term, is not the leader who has been following Christ for years, but the new Christian who is learning to be a disciple-maker from the ground up.

Some use the adjective *viral* to describe this kind of growth, as illustrated by the book *Viral Churches*, by Ed Stetzer and Warren Bird. Movements take on a life of their own much like a virus, expanding in new and creative ways. Epidemiology, the study of the factors that influence the spread of disease, can help us understand how the gospel spreads through a movement. This is a topic which the world has experienced firsthand through the COVID-19 pandemic, but a deeper understanding of how diseases spread can help us understand the principle of the end user and why we emphasize reproducibility. Epidemiologists have identified key factors that determine how a specific disease will spread. These factors can be identified by five basic questions:

- Question #1: *How serious is the disease?* This measures the degree to which the disease changes a person's life. Something like the common cold has very little impact, but some viruses have proven to be life-threatening or have a long-term impact.

- Question #2: *How contagious is the disease?* The easier the disease is to transmit, the more it will be caught by others.

- Question #3: *What is the duration of infection?* The longer a person is sick with a specific disease, the more exposure he will have to others, which means that more people will be infected with it.

- Question #4: *How infected is the person with the disease?* The more a disease impacts a person, the more likely it is to infect others.

- Question #5: *How many people are exposed to those who are infected by the disease?*[1]

Of course, this is a simplistic explanation of a complex issue, as every disease has unique issues that influence how it spreads through a population. However, these five questions provide a basic introduction that can help us understand the way the gospel spreads in a movement. Notice that all the questions pertain to a recently infected person reproducing that infection in others. They are not questions about the disease's origins or if it is spreading from a coordinated center. The questions are seeking to identify how the disease takes on a life of its own in a newly infected person, because diseases reproduce at the fringes, not from a home base.

Therefore, unlike a disease where the goal is to decrease each of these factors, the goal in a movement is to do everything possible to increase them. Let's consider each of these questions in turn:[2]

- Question #1: *How serious is the gospel to the new disciple?* This is about eternal life, a serious issue for most people. One time I was in a meeting with twenty-five former Imams, and I asked them why they became disciple-makers of Jesus Christ. "For eternal life" was the dominant answer. These are thinking people who realize that that they would eventually face their mortality and that had concerns about what came after that.

  Therefore, for most of the people in our movements, repentance and baptism is a serious issue. It goes against the flow of the majority culture, and all face some form of persecution because of their conversion. We do not water down the meaning of the gospel in any way to get more converts. The cost of discipleship is evident to all.

---

1 Hayward, "Mathematical Modeling of Church Growth."
2 Hayward.

- Question #2: *How contagious is the gospel through the new disciple-maker?* The new disciple has had a fresh encounter with the love of God, resulting in what the Bible refers to as a "first love." Instead of waiting for the new convert to level out, we fan the flame of this first love, encouraging them to share what has happened to them with family and friends. This first experience of hope, grace, and forgiveness through Jesus sets them free from the guilt of the law—a life-changing, transformative experience for all.

- Question #3: *What is the duration of infection?* In our experience, if the new disciple is immediately empowered and encouraged to make disciple-makers through the 5-5-5 system, this "first love" can last for years. We have seen almost all converts share their faith and engage in house churches, overcome persecutions, and become obedient disciples of Jesus. Many go on to initiate new networks of disciple-makers, some starting five or even a dozen or more networks, while working full time and caring for a family. Few are financially supported or compensated for their sacrificial lifestyles, except by joy, fruitfulness, and the power of the Holy Spirit in their lives.

- Question #4: *How infected is the new disciple with the gospel?* We have found that the level of impact that the gospel has on the life of the new disciple is influenced by the way that the gospel comes to them. Some have supernatural encounters with Christ through dreams or visions. Many are healed of an illness and experience the presence and power of the Holy Spirit in their lives in an extraordinary way. All have an encounter with the living Word of Christ, the gospel being shared in a way that they "hear" and have a transformative experience with the life of Jesus.

  Not all are impacted like the Apostle Paul on the road to Damascus, but all receive the Word implanted in them with faith and are energized by the hope of salvation and the love of Jesus. When this gospel is shared by a trusted family member or friend, the doors of their hearts often swing wide open to the presence and power of the Holy Spirit. No one is "joining a church" for social reasons, in light of the persecutions that will surely come. All are significantly impacted.

- Question #5: *How many people are exposed to those impacted by the gospel?* I just received a testimony of a disciple who works in a brick yard, one of the lowest levels of employment available. Many times they are paid with food rather than cash. This brother shared his faith with a customer, who heard the story of Jesus's sacrifice on the cross for him and responded by saying that he never knew that one person would die for his sins.

He returned home and told the story to his wife, who became so excited that she shared with over forty family and friends. The disciple-maker visited the family a few days later and found forty-two people ready to receive baptism and become disciple-makers. How many are exposed? This question will only be answerable in eternity.

The Principle of Releasing Disciple-Makers

An absolute essential for fostering reproduction is allowing everyone—yes, everyone—to lead, because everyone is a disciple-maker. We build this into the process from day one of the journey of the new Christian. This is a key to understanding how the 5-5-5 system works. Let's look at the various components of the system that make reproduction practical.

The 5-5-5 System

As I stated in chapter 8, we ask every new disciple to reach five family members and friends with the gospel. Those who have shared their faith in Jesus also mentor the new convert to identify people in their lives with whom they can share. Some basic Scriptures are taught that they can easily memorize. They already know what happened to them and how they were impacted by Jesus's love, so they simply reproduce this. It is a simple, reproducible process that everyone can do.

> Because these 5-5-5 networks are organic, relational, and decentralized—as opposed to being organized by a centralized structure—they do not require a complex system to develop.

Remember the principle of the mother duck and her brood following in a line behind her. As he or she shares with five and baptizes them, he is also challenging them and helping each of the five to impart the gospel to five each. There is friendship, love, and mentoring that produce joy and hope and changed lives. This can sound perfunctory when written in black and white, however, we are talking about transforming the lives of millions of people.

Because these 5-5-5 networks are organic, relational, and decentralized—as opposed to being organized by a centralized structure—they do not require a complex system to develop. Spontaneous growth happens and the simplicity of the gospel and the joy of changed lives producing hope and meaning in a stressful and discouraging world develops people who joyfully share their experience with others.

The Church Meetings

Movement churches are simple house churches of at least six baptized believers. They are streamlined, and therefore everyone is freed up to lead them because they are organic churches that do not depend on buildings, budgets, and profession clergy. The meetings will range from an hour to several hours long, depending on the circumstances. In many cases, new believers will host the meeting and leadership may be shared between the participants. The meeting could consist of a handful of men sitting under a tree or a dozen adults and children crammed into a small home or apartment. The exact form is not prescribed. The form fits the life of the group members, so that they meet in a way that works for their situation.

We support those who lead these meetings by providing discussion guides, which were introduced in chapter 10. They are written in such a way that an oral learner who has a family member or friend who is literate can easily relate to the stories that are told and discuss the Scriptures that are shared.

Each lesson is designed to discuss a Bible passage, figure out how to apply it in their own context, and encourage each other in obedience. Many house churches are led by oral learners, and their members are all oral learners. The Bible stories and application can be passed down by a mentor through songs and dramas created by the house church members and various other methods appropriate to the context.

Learning Communities

The leaders of house churches participate in Learning Communities (see chapter 9), where a 5-5-5 leader guides them through the discussion guides. In the LC, the group walks through the Bible discussions together and has firsthand experience that they can easily repeat in their house-church meetings. In fact, whatever they do in the Learning Community meetings is done in a way to empower the leaders to reproduce this experience in their house churches. This is a just-in-time learning process instead of the just-in-case learning model. The just-in-time is provided at the time of need, and the just-in-case is what we do when we go to school and learn various methods.

Baptism and Communion

If you are led to Christ by a new disciple who was baptized by a friend or relative and who is seeking to reach their first five people, then you will be baptized by that person, not an ordained professional who went to Bible school to learn how to baptize. I know that I've said this many times in this book, but because this practice is so ingrained in our typical leadership practices, it bears repeating. We do not want a credentialed person to lead or perform the baptism. We empower everyone to baptize, making the process as simple as possible.

Some might interpret what we do as making light of this crucial sign of the Christian faith. However, you must understand that water baptism in these contexts is already viewed as significant. As stated previously, many local people don't care if individuals believe in Christ, but they do object if they are baptized. The majority religion views baptism as an act of rejection of other religions and of commitment to Jesus Christ alone. Baptism is a public sign of their faith, which the new believer takes seriously, and it often results in pushback and persecution. We don't want to create any barriers to helping people make this public confession of Jesus by making them wait for someone who is "officially qualified" to perform it.

> Baptism is a public sign of their faith, which the new believer takes seriously, and it often results in pushback and persecution.

The same is true of sharing communion. We facilitate simple experiences of remembering the death and resurrection of Jesus that don't require the presence of clergy or any of the complicating trappings. We share the body and blood of Christ at various training events and in Learning Communities in a way that can be repeated in house churches.

Conclusion

A basic question we often ask is this: Can this experience be repeated at the most basic level of the church? This means that whatever we do must be able to be repeated by a house-church leader or a new Christian who is seeking to reach his or her five. If we are doing something at a leadership level that requires an expert, we think it through. Is there a simpler way to do this, or teach this, that is easily reproducible by a new disciple-maker?

People repeat what they see and experience. That's just a natural way of learning. If a leader lectures for an hour, then people will think that becoming a leader means that they too must give such lectures in order to lead. We don't tell people what to do and how to do it. We show them.

In order to facilitate the work of the Holy Spirit, we shape everything that happens with leaders so that they are easily reproduced by the local, grassroots person in his own context within his own resources. If it is costly or complex, it is avoided. Even if we have a training event that is delivered outside of their local environment, we design it so that grassroots individuals experience it in a way that they can repeat in their own networks. With this mindset, reproduction is the natural outcome.

Chapter 14

Next Steps

Where do you go from here? The answer to this question depends on where you are on the movement learning curve. It isn't a simple thing to make the shift from our Western church paradigm to movement thinking. I have found it to be one of the most challenging paradigm shifts in all of life. For those of us who have lived in the first world and been educated here, acquiring, manipulating, and applying knowledge makes us "knowledge workers." Culturally, we tend to treat Christianity and the church with the same perspective. However, movement work requires a deeper dive into how the Holy Spirit works in us and how he works in the lives of unbelievers, along with a humble curiosity about cultures unlike our own.

> Movements flow through social connections in these *we* cultures, as the Spirit touches groups of people in ways that are hard to fathom in contexts where we tend to solely focus on individuals.

This is not a challenge to become an expert in cultural anthropology, as some have required. But we do need to realize the basic differences between cultures. For example, in the West, people first think with a focus on *me*. In many other cultures, the focus is on *we* and relationships, not individuals. Movements flow through social connections in these *we* cultures, as the Spirit touches groups of people in ways that are hard to fathom in contexts where we tend to solely focus on individuals. I find it hard not to write about this more as I conclude this book, because it is so foundational. At this point, it is enough to say that the principles outlined in chapter 7 are important, whether you are a movement novice or have been involved in movements for ten years.

To build upon this foundation of the work of the Spirit in relational cultures, let me provide concrete direction to both the novice and the experienced leader. If you are new to this conversation, realize that there are a variety of perspectives. I suggest that you do a Google search on the topics and authors that I have referred to in this book. Immerse yourself in the literature and the trainings that have been developed. When you are learning a new topic, repetition is crucial. You need exposure to these ideas so that you embrace the new imagination about how God works in movements. My first book, *Movements That Move*, outlines basic proven principles that work in different contexts. I also suggest that you work with at least one other person on movement research and reading. You will need to process what you are learning in order to make the necessary shifts.

The organization 24:14 provides one of the best ways to help you network with others on the same journey (www.2414now.net/). This is a comprehensive website, as many people around the world connect here. Another great resource to learn movement basics online is Zumé Training (www.zume.training/training). If you want to dig deeper, Curtis Sergeant's Meta Camp (www.metacamp.org) will provide a hands-on, face-to-face training opportunity like no other. Steve Addison's website (www.movements. net) is excellent for learning more about the movement community and for great ideas. Other good resources for learning about movements are Biglife (www.big.life) and New Generations (www.newgenerations.org).

For those of you who are already deeply engaged in movement work, it is important to ask where you are in this process. I have talked to many who have seen initial success in getting a movement off the ground, but now they are seeking how to make it sustainable and long-lasting. How does one shift from an upstart movement to one that expands to four hundred generations? Some might challenge the legitimacy of this question. They argue that we must focus on the sovereignty of God and assume that if he wants it to last, it will last. Our role is only to be a catalyst and move on, since this is what the Apostle Paul did. We shouldn't focus on the longevity of movements, because none of the churches in the New Testament still exists today.

> It is my goal that these movements will continue to reproduce for many generations and avoid the trap of becoming institutionalized and lose the dynamic of the Holy Spirit's inspiration for reproduction.

I think we can agree that God's concern, as expressed in 2 Peter 3:9, is that "he is patient with you, not wanting anyone to perish, but everyone to come to repentance." The purpose of movements is to reach as many people with the saving grace of Jesus Christ as possible, not to establish churches that will last until the Lord's return. Having said that, however, it is my goal that these movements will continue to reproduce for many generations and avoid the trap of becoming institutionalized and lose the dynamic of the Holy Spirit's inspiration for reproduction.

All around us we see that tradition and human goals seem to dominate our organizations and even lead some Christian leaders to walk away from the biblical guidelines for living holy lives. Living in humble recognition of his purposes for mankind to make disciple-makers, as expressed in what we know as the Great Commission, can and will continue the growth on the edges of movements for many generations.

I have outlined how we are seeing in fifteen years of movement work in Southeast Asia and West Africa the results of sustainable movement expansion. Will these movements last for multiple generations, with a generation being defined as thirty to forty years? Only the Lord knows, but it seems to me that the Spirit is poured out for a period of time, not indefinitely, in seasons of rapid growth and multiplication of disciples. Many, if not most, mission leaders would agree that this is happening now in the Muslim world and in other unreached places, as we see a pattern of signs and wonders, dreams and visions, and the revelation of Christ in the hearts of many.

Our responsibility is to be like the men of Issachar in 1 Chronicles 12:32: " ... from Issachar, men who understood the times and knew what Israel should do." We have our marching orders: the Great Commission to make disciple-makers. Jesus was very clear, saying that "this gospel of the kingdom will be preached in the whole world as a testimony to all nations, and then the end will come" (Matt 24:14). Let's join what God is doing, as his Spirit is touching hearts and lives, and reach the masses of people with his eternal love.

> He wrote about the principle of "doing the right things" instead of just "doing things right."

As we go out to all ethnic groups of the world to initiate, facilitate, and catalyze movements, let's focus on doing the right things, not on doing things right. This was an emphasis of the great Christian leader, Peter Drucker, about whom Pastor Rick Warren, the founding pastor of Saddleback Church in Lake Forrest, California, said:

> "I'm often embarrassed at how often I quote Peter Drucker," Warren said. "He had a way of saying things simply. Peter was far more than the founder of modern management, far more than a brilliant man, one of the greatest minds of the 20th century. He was a great soul. If I summed up Peter's life in three words, it would be integrity, humility and generosity. ... Peter was the only truly Renaissance man I've ever known. He had a way of looking at the world in a systems view that said it all matters."[1]

In the 1990s, Drucker's book, *The Effective Executive*, changed my life. He wrote about the principle of "doing the right things" instead of just

---

1 Ostdick, "Peter Drucker: The Father of Management Theory."

"doing things right." Of course we want to please God and live a godly life, but this focus can be a trap when we embrace human traditions or old mission methods that don't produce the good fruit of the kingdom of God and place theological constraints around them. Our focus is to be upon "doing the right things," and movements are the "right things" to be focusing on as we, like the men of Issachar, "understand our times and know what we should do." In fact, this idea was the springboard for my six-year research project to determine "the right things to do in movements," and the resulting seven root principles that have propelled our movement work.

In this book I have tried to give both historical perspectives and contemporary examples of the right things to do to initiate movements in the early stages and to sustain them over the long haul. There are hundreds, if not thousands, of newly-minted movements around the world today.

Obviously, as learners we need to look broadly at what God is teaching his people about how to build movements that last. I am confident that if you will evaluate what you plan to do, or are currently doing, in the light of the practices presented in this book and in *Movements That Move*, you will have the basis for laying the foundation of movements that will expand generationally and endure through the work of his Spirit and the life found in the Word of God.

May the Lord richly bless you with "a hearing heart" and wisdom to obey what he teaches you. May he do above and beyond all that you ask, imagine, or desire, according to his will and for his glory!

Bibliography

Adeney, Miriam. *Daughters of Islam: Building Bridges with Muslim Women*. Downers Grove, IL: InterVarsity Press, 2009.

Albert, Eleanor. "Christianity in China." Council on Foreign Relations website. Last updated October 11, 2018. https://www.cfr.org/backgrounder/christianity-china.

Allen, Roland. *The Compulsion of the Spirit: A Roland Allen Reader*. Grand Rapids: Eerdmans, 1983.

Allen, Roland. *Missionary Methods: St. Paul's or Ours?* Grand Rapids: Eerdmans, 1962.

Allen, Roland. *The Spontaneous Expansion of the Church and the Causes Which Hinder It*. Grand Rapids: Eerdmans, 1962.

Bach, Eugene, and Brother Zhu. *The Underground Church*. New Kensington, PA: Whitaker House, 2014.

Banks, Robert. *Paul's Idea of Community*. Peabody, MA: Hendrickson Publishers, 1994.

Banks, Robert, and Julia Banks. *The Church Comes Home: A New Base for Community and Mission*. Australia: Albatros Books, 1986.

Barabási, Albert-László. *Linked: How Everything Is Connected to Everything Else and What It Means for Business, Science, and Everyday Life*. New York: Basic Books, 2014.

Barth, Markus, *Ephesians 4–6*. Garden City, NY: Doubleday, 1974.

Brafman, Ori, and Rod A. Beckstrom. *The Starfish and the Spider: The Unstoppable Power of Leaderless Organizations*. New York: Portfolio, 2006.

Bright, Bill. "Your Personal Guide to Fasting and Prayer." Cru website. Accessed April 23, 2022. https://www.cru.org/us/en/train-and-grow/spiritual-growth/fasting/personal-guide-to-fasting.html.

Chan, Francis. *Letters to the Church*. Colorado Springs: David C. Cook, 2018.

Clark, Andrew D. *Serve the Community of the Church*. Grand Rapids: Eerdmans, 2000.

Cole, Neil. *Church 3.0: Upgrades for the Future of the Church*. Leadership Network. San Francisco: Jossey-Bass, 2010.

Cooke, Tony. "John Wesley Saw Some Crazy Miracles!" *Destiny Image*. November 6, 2020. https://www.destinyimage.com/blog/tony-cooke-john-wesely-experienced-incredible-holy-spirit-manifestations.

Corbett, Steven, and Brian Fikkert. *When Helping Hurts: How to Alleviate Poverty without Hurting the Poor … and Yourself*. Chicago: Moody Publishers, 2012.

Covey, Stephen R. *The Eighth Habit*. New York: Free Press, 2005.

DuFour, Richard, and Robert Eaker. *Professional Learning Communities at Work: Best Practices for Enhancing Student Achievement*. Bloomington, IN: National Educational Service, 1998.

Dunn, James D. G. *Beginning from Jerusalem: Christianity in the Making, Vol. 2.* Grand Rapids: Eerdmans, 2020.

Farah, Warrick, ed. *Motus Dei: The Movement of God to Disciple the Nations*. Littleton, CO: William Carey Publishing, 2021.

Finger, Ria Halterman. *Of Widows and Meals: Communal Meals in the Book of Acts*. Grand Rapids: Eerdmans, 2007.

Garrison, David. *Church Planting Movements: How God Is Redeeming a Lost World*. Midlothian, VA: WIGTake Resources, 2004.

Garrison, David. *A Wind in the House of Islam: How God Is Drawing Muslims around the World to Faith in Jesus Christ*. Monument, CO: WIGTake Resources, 2014.

Gehring, Roger W. *House Church and Mission: The Importance of Household Structures in Early Christianity*. Peabody, MA: Hendrickson Publishers, 2004.

Giles, Kevin. *Patterns of Ministry among the First Christians*. Melbourne, Australia: Collins Dove, 1989.

Gilovich, Thomas. "Seeing the Past in the Future: The Effect of Associations to Familiar Events on Judgments and Decisions." *Journal of Personality and Social Psychology* 40, no. 5 (1981): 797–808.

Global Frontier Missions website. "Church Planting Movements (CPMs) and Disciple Making Movements (DMMs)." Accessed January 28, 2023. https://globalfrontiermissions.o rg/church-planting/church-planting-movements-cpms-and-disciple-making-movements-dmms/.

Goodhart, Charles. "Problems of Monetary Management: The U.K. Experience." In *Inflation, Depression, and Economic Policy in the West*, edited by Anthony S. Courakis, 91–121. Totowa, NJ: Barnes and Noble Books, 1981.

Green, Michael. *Evangelism in the Early Church*. Grand Rapids: Eerdmans, 1970.

Hawkins, Greg L., and Cally Parkinson. *REVEAL: Where Are You?* Barrington, IL: Willow Creek Resources, 2007.

Hayward, John. "Mathematical Modeling of Church Growth." *Journal of Mathematical Sociology* 26 (August 2010): 255–92. 1999.

Hellerman, Joseph. *When the Church Was a Family*. Nashville: B&H Academic, 2009.

Hodges, Melvin. *The Indigenous Church*. Ventura, CA: Gospel Publishing House, 2012.

John, Victor, with David Coles. *Bhojpuri Breakthrough: A Movement That Keeps Multiplying*. Monument, CO: WIGTake Resources, 2019.

Kai, Ying, and Grace Kai. *Training for Trainers: The Movement That Changed the World*. Monument, CO: WIGTake Resources, 2018.

Kim, Daniel. "Introduction to Systems Thinking." The Systems Thinker. April 19, 2023. www.thesystemsthinker.com.

Knight, William. *Memoir of the Rev. H. Venn: The Missionary Secretariat of Henry Venn, B.D., Prebendary of St. Paul's, and Honorary Secretary of the Church Missionary Society*. London: Longmans, Green and Co., 1880.

Kreider, Alan. *The Patient Ferment of the Early Church: The Improbable Rise of Christianity in the Roman Empire*. Grand Rapids: Baker Academic, 2016.

Marquet, L. David. *Turn the Ship Around: A True Story of Turning Followers into Leaders*. New York: Penguin Random House, 2012.

McGavran, Donald A. *The Bridges of God*. London: World Dominion Press, 1955.

McGavran, Donald A. *Ethnic Realities and the Church: Lessons from India*. Pasadena, CA: William Carey Publishing, 1979.

McGavran, Donald A. *Momentous Decisions in Missions Today*. Grand Rapids: Baker, 1984.

McGavran, Donald A., and Win Arn. *How to Grow a Church*. Ventura, CA: Regal Books, 1973.

McGavran, Donald A., and C. Peter Wagner. *Understanding Church Growth*. 3rd ed. Grand Rapids: Eerdmans, 1990.

Moran, Roy. *Spent Matches: Igniting the Signal Fire for the Spiritually Dissatisfied*. Nashville: Thomas Nelson, 2015.

Neill, Steven. *A History of Christian Missions*. New York: Penguin Books, 1964.

Nevius, John. *The Planting and Development of Missionary Churches*. New York: Foreign Missionary Library, 2015.

Osiek, Carolyn, and David Balch. *Families in the New Testament World*. Louisville: John Knox Press, 1997.

Ostdick, John H. "Peter Drucker: The Father of Management Theory." SUCCESS. com. June 8, 2010. https://www.success.com/peter-drucker-the-father-of-management-theory/.

Patzia, Arthur. *The Emergence of the Church: Context, Growth, Leadership & Worship*. Downers Grove, IL: IVP Academic, 2001.

Payne, J. D., ed. *Roland Allen's Ministry of Expansion*. Pasadena, CA: William Carey Publishing, 2017.

Pickett, J. W., D. A. McGavran, J. W. Warnshuis, and G. H. Singh. *Church Growth and Group Conversion*. Pasadena, CA: William Carey Library, 1973.

Reach, Robert M. *Movements That Move: 7 Root Principles That Nurture Church Planting Movements*. Apple Valley, MN: ChurchSmart Resources, 2016.

Saban, Nick, and Brian Curtis. *How Good Do You Want To Be: A Champion's Tips on How To Lead and Succeed at Work and in Life*. New York: Ballantine Books, 2007.

Sanneh, Lamin. "Introductory Essay." In *The Ministry of the Spirit: Selected Writings of Roland Allen*. Edited by David M. Paton. Cambridge: Lutterworth Press, 2006.

Schwarz, Christian A. *Natural Church Development: A Guide to Eight Essential Qualities of Healthy Churches*. Carol Stream, IL: ChurchSmart Resources, 1996.

Sergeant, Curtis. *The Only One: Living Fully In, By, and For God*. Littleton, CO: William Carey Publishing, 2019.

Sessoms, Rick. *Leading with Story: Cultivating Christ-Centered Leaders in a Storycentric Generation*. Pasadena, CA: William Carey Library, 2016.

Shenk, Wilbert. "The Contribution of Henry Venn to Mission Thought." *Anvil* 2, no. 1 (1985): 25–42.

Smith, Steve, and Ying Kai. *T4T: A Discipleship Re-Revolution*. Monument, CO: WIGTake Resources, 2011.

Stark, Rodney. *The Rise of Christianity: How the Obscure, Marginal Jesus Movement Became the Dominant Religious Force in the Western World in a Few Centuries*. San Francisco: HarperSanFrancisco, 1997.

Stetzer, Ed, and Thom S. Rainer. *Transformational Church: Creating a New Scorecard for Congregations*. Nashville: B&H Publishing, 2010.

Trousdale, Jerry. *Miraculous Movements: How Hundreds of Thousands of Muslims Are Falling in Love with Jesus*. Nashville: Thomas Nelson, 2012.

Watson, David L., and Paul D. Watson. *Contagious Disciple Making: Leading Others on a Journey of Discovery*. Nashville: Thomas Nelson, 2014.

Wright, N. T. *Jesus and the Victory of God*. Christian Origins and the Question of God, vol. 2. Minneapolis: Fortress Press, 1997.

Xi, Lian. *Redeemed by Fire: The Rise of Popular Christianity in Modern China*. New Haven: Yale University Press, 2010.

Appendix

A Comprehensive Listing of References to Jesus ('Isa) in the Qur'an

Among the major world religions, Islam is the only non-Christian faith that recognizes the person of Jesus. Qur'an talks a great amount about Jesus.

However, Jesus Christ is the most controversial personality in Islam. In the Qur'an, Jesus is referred to in over ninety verses in fifteen surahs. Islam corroborates that Jesus was born to a virgin, was sinless, performed miracles, and was superior to other prophets. Yet, Islam teaches that Jesus was no more than a prophet. It denies the central message of Christianity by denying Jesus's divinity, crucifixion, and resurrection.

Surah Reference (Yusufali translation)

2:87   We gave Jesus the son of Mary Clear (Signs) and strengthened him with the holy spirit.

2:136   We believe in Allah, and the revelation given to us, and to Abraham, Isma'il, Isaac, Jacob, and the Tribes, and that given to Moses and Jesus, and that given to (all) prophets from their Lord: We make no difference between one and another of them ...

2:253   ... To Jesus the son of Mary We gave clear (Signs), and strengthened him with the holy spirit.

3:45   O Mary! Allah giveth thee glad tidings of a Word from Him: his name will be Christ Jesus, the son of Mary, held in honour in this world and the Hereafter and of (the company of) those nearest to Allah.

3:46   "He shall speak to the people in childhood and in maturity. And he shall be (of the company) of the righteous."

3:48   And Allah will teach him the Book and Wisdom, the Law and the Gospel.

3:49   And (appoint him) a messenger to the Children of Israel, (with this message): "I have come to you, with a Sign from your Lord, in that I make for you out of clay, as it were, the figure of a bird, and breathe into it, and it becomes a bird by Allah's leave: And I heal those born blind, and the lepers, and I quicken the dead, by Allah's leave; and I declare to you what ye eat, and what ye store in your houses. Surely therein is a Sign for you if ye did believe."

3:50   (I have come to you), to attest the Law which was before me. And to make lawful to you part of what was (Before) forbidden to you; I have come to you with a Sign from your Lord. So fear Allah, and obey me.

3:52   When Jesus found Unbelief on their part He said: "Who will be My helpers to (the work of) Allah?"

3:55   Behold! Allah said: "O Jesus! I will take thee and raise thee to Myself and clear thee (of the falsehoods) of those who blaspheme; I will make those who follow thee superior to those who reject faith, to the Day of Resurrection: Then shall ye all return unto me, and I will judge between you of the matters wherein ye dispute."

3:59   The similitude of Jesus before Allah is as that of Adam …

3:84   … and in (the Books) given to Moses, Jesus, and the prophets, from their Lord.

4:157   That they said (in boast), "We killed Christ Jesus the son of Mary, the Messenger of Allah;" but they killed him not, nor crucified him, but so it was made to appear to them, and those who differ therein are full of doubts, with no (certain) knowledge, but only conjecture to follow, for of a surety they killed him not.

4:163   We have sent thee inspiration, as We sent it to Noah and the Messengers after him: we sent inspiration to Abraham, Isma'il, Isaac, Jacob and the Tribes, to Jesus, Job, Jonah, Aaron, and Solomon, and to David We gave the Psalms.

4:171   O People of the Book! Commit no excesses in your religion: Nor say of Allah aught but the truth. Christ Jesus the son of Mary was (no more than) a messenger of Allah, and His Word, which He bestowed on Mary, and a spirit proceeding from Him: so believe in Allah and His messengers. Say not "Trinity": desist: it will be better for you: for Allah is one Allah: Glory be to Him: (far exalted is He) above having a son. To Him belong all things in the heavens and on earth.

4:172   Christ disdaineth nor to serve and worship Allah …

5:17   In blasphemy indeed are those that say that Allah is Christ the son of Mary.

5:46   And in their footsteps We sent Jesus the son of Mary, confirming the Law that had come before him: We sent him the Gospel: therein was guidance and light, and confirmation of the Law that had come before him: a guidance and an admonition to those who fear Allah.

5:72   They do blaspheme who say: "Allah is Christ the son of Mary." But said Christ: "O Children of Israel! worship Allah, my Lord and your Lord." Whoever joins other gods with Allah, Allah will forbid him the garden, and the Fire will be his abode.

5:75   Christ the son of Mary was no more than a messenger; many were the messengers that passed away before him. His mother was a woman of truth. They had both to eat their (daily) food.

5:78   Curses were pronounced on those among the Children of Israel who rejected Faith, by the tongue of David and of Jesus the son of Mary: because they disobeyed and persisted in excesses.

5:110   O Jesus the son of Mary! Recount My favour to thee and to thy mother. Behold! I strengthened thee with the holy spirit, so that thou didst speak to the people in childhood and in maturity. Behold! I taught thee the Book and Wisdom, the Law and the Gospel and behold! thou makest out of clay, as it were, the figure of a bird, by My leave, and thou breathest into it and it becometh a bird by My leave, and thou healest those born blind, and the lepers, by My leave. And behold! thou bringest forth the dead by My leave. And behold! I did restrain the Children of Israel from (violence to) thee when thou didst show them the clear Signs, and the unbelievers among them said: "This is nothing but evident magic."

5:112   Behold! the disciples, said: "O Jesus the son of Mary! can thy Lord send down to us a table set (with viands) from heaven?" Said Jesus: "Fear Allah, if ye have faith."

5:114   Said Jesus the son of Mary: "O Allah our Lord! Send us from heaven a table set (with viands), that there may be for us for the first and the last of us a solemn festival and a sign from thee; and provide for our sustenance, for thou art the best Sustainer (of our needs)."

5:116   Allah will say: "O Jesus the son of Mary! Didst thou say unto men, worship me and my mother as gods in derogation of Allah?" He will say: "Glory to Thee! never could I say what I had no right (to say). Had I said such a thing, thou wouldst indeed have known it. Thou knowest what is in my heart ..."

6:85   And Zakariya and John, and Jesus and Elias: all in the ranks of the righteous.

9:30   The Jews call Uzair a son of Allah, and the Christians call Christ the son of Allah.

9:31   They take their priests and their anchorites to be their lords in derogation of Allah, and (they take as their Lord) Christ the son of Mary; yet they were commanded to worship but One Allah: there is no god but He. Praise and glory to Him: (Far is He) from having the partners they associate (with Him).

19:19   He said: "Nay, I am only a messenger from thy Lord, (to announce) to thee the gift of a holy son."

19:20   She said: "How shall I have a son, seeing that no man has touched me, and I am not unchaste?"

19:21   He said: "So (it will be): Thy Lord saith, 'that is easy for Me: and (We wish) to appoint him as a Sign unto men and a Mercy from Us': It is a matter (so) decreed."

19:22   So she conceived him, and she retired with him to a remote place.

19:27   At length she brought the (babe) to her people, carrying him (in her arms). They said: "O Mary! truly an amazing thing hast thou brought!"

19:30   He said: "I am indeed a servant of Allah: He hath given me revelation and made me a prophet."

19:31   "And He hath made me blessed wheresoever I be, and hath enjoined on me Prayer and Charity as long as I live."

19:32   "(He) hath made me kind to my mother, and not overbearing or miserable."

19:33   "So peace is on me the day I was born, the day that I die, and the day that I shall be raised up to life (again)!"

19:34   Such (was) Jesus the son of Mary: (it is) a statement of truth, about which they (vainly) dispute.

19:88   They say: "(Allah) Most Gracious has begotten a son!"

19:91   That they should invoke a son for (Allah) Most Gracious.

19:92   For it is not consonant with the majesty of (Allah) Most Gracious that He should beget a son.

21:91   And (remember) her who guarded her chastity: We breathed into her of Our spirit, and We made her and her son a sign for all peoples.

23:50   And We made the son of Mary and his mother as a Sign: We gave them both shelter on high ground, affording rest and security and furnished with springs.

33:7   And remember We took from the prophets their covenant: As (We did) from thee: from Noah, Abraham, Moses, and Jesus the son of Mary: We took from them a solemn covenant.

42:13   The same religion has He established for you as that which He enjoined on Noah the which We have sent by inspiration to thee and that which We enjoined on Abraham, Moses, and Jesus: Namely, that ye should remain steadfast in religion, and make no divisions therein: to those who worship other things than Allah, hard is the (way) to which thou callest them.

Allah chooses to Himself those whom He pleases, and guides to Himself those who turn (to Him).

43:57   When (Jesus) the son of Mary is held up as an example, behold, thy people raise a clamour thereat (in ridicule)!

43:61   And (Jesus) shall be a Sign (for the coming of) the Hour (of Judgment): therefore have no doubt about the (Hour), but follow ye Me: this is a Straight Way.

43:63   When Jesus came with Clear Signs, he said: "Now have I come to you with Wisdom, and in order to make clear to you some of the (points) on which ye dispute: therefore fear Allah and obey me."

57:27   We sent after them Jesus the son of Mary, and bestowed on him the Gospel; and We ordained in the hearts of those who followed him Compassion and Mercy ...

61:6   And remember, Jesus, the son of Mary, said: "O Children of Israel! I am the messenger of Allah (sent) to you, confirming the Law (which came) before me, and giving Glad Tidings of a Messenger to come after me, whose name shall be Ahmad." But when he came to them with Clear Signs, they said, "this is evident sorcery!"

61:14   O ye who believe! Be ye helpers of Allah: As said Jesus the son of Mary to the Disciples, "Who will be my helpers to (the work of) Allah?" Said the disciples, "We are Allah's helpers!" then a portion of the Children of Israel believed, and a portion disbelieved: But We gave power to those who believed, against their enemies, and they became the ones that prevailed.

N. S. R. K. Ravi

WILLIAM CAREY PUBLISHING

visit us at missionbooks.org

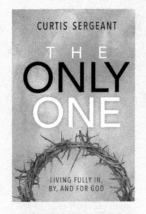

The Only One: Living Fully In, By, and For God

Curtis Sergeant | Paperback & ePub

Designed to be read, processed, shared, and used to equip others, *The Only One* is a tool to not only grow as a disciple but also to make and multiply disciples. This is about living with a greater impact on the world and the purpose for which God designed you. It's time to experience life with Him, and others, as a joyful and exciting adventure— read this book and get started!

Mobilizing Movements: Leadership Insights for Discipling Whole Nations

Murray Moerman | Paperback & ePub

Moerman provides realistic expectations of what it takes to facilitate a movement and how to gain the support of various partners needed for long-term success, resulting in whole-nation church planting saturation. Based on years of research, *Mobilizing Movements* contains both practical and spiritual elements. You will find insights and models from several continents for macro (whole nation) strategies and micro (personal) disciple-making.

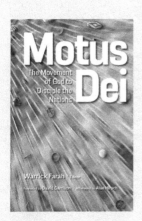

Motus Dei: The Movement of God to Disciple the Nations

Warrick Farah, editor | Paperback & ePub

Motus Dei locates the current Church Planting Movement (CPM) phenomenon within modern history, while tracing its roots back to the first century, and articulates a missiological description of the dynamics of Disciple Making Movements (DMMs) in Asia, Africa, and diaspora contexts in the Global North. Offering over thirty first-hand accounts of indigenous churches planting churches among the nations, *Motus Dei* provides a seedbed for growing movements in diverse contexts.